I Can't See the Azaleas

True Crimes Against Women and Children

By

Dianna Cook Thomas

This book is a work of non-fiction. Names and places have been changed to protect the privacy of all individuals. The events and situations are true.

© 2003, 2014 by Dianna Cook Thomas. All rights reserved.

No part of this book may be reproduced, stored in a retrieval system, or transmitted by any means, electronic, mechanical, photocopying, recording, or otherwise, without written permission from the author.

ISBN: 978-1-4140-1551-4 (sc)
ISBN: 978-1-4140-1550-7 (hc)
ISBN: 978-1-4140-1552-1 (e)

Library of Congress Control Number: 2003098193

1stBooks - rev. 10/28/03

All Scripture quotations contained herein, unless otherwise noted, are taken from the "Holy Bible, New International Version."® Copyright©1973, 1978, 1984 by International Bible Society. Used by permission of Zondervan Publishing House. All rights reserved.

The "NIV" and "New International Version" trademarks are registered in the United States Patent and Trademark Office by International Bible Society. Use of either trademark requires the permission of International Bible Society.

              Photography by Roger Courtney
                 www.roger-courtney.com

Dedication

I dedicate this book to the Lord, my family, and all my friends from the Shreveport Police Department. To other agencies who helped me and shared their information so willingly, I say thank you. It is also to the women and children who have died a violent death, or suffered greatly at the hands of another, that I dedicate this work.

A special thanks goes to Margaret Carmouche, Kacee Hargrave, Debra Jacobs, Patricia Roberts, Mark Rogers, Garry Bass, Patricia Lamotte, Martha Matlock, Noble Cook, Albert Thomas, Roger Courtney, Suzanne Gallier, Benevolent Funeral Home, Eric Brock, and my Aunt Luverdia.

In Loving Memory of my Brother Jonathan Brian Cook

Content

Preface: The Beauty of an Azalea xi
Introduction xiii

    I'm Too Young 1
    I'm Too Pretty 17
    I'm Too Ugly 27
    I Can Live Again! 35
    I'm Too Smart 43
    I'm Smart Enough To Discipline and Train My
       Children 53
    I'm Smart Enough To Avoid Infant Abuse 59
    I'm Smart Enough Not To Drink and Drive 67
    I'm Too Rich 79
    But I Trust Him 83
    I Have a Financially Secure Future 109
    I'm Too Old 117
    Profiling 123
    Crime Prevention 129

Conclusion 139
About the Author 145

Preface

The Beauty of an Azalea

    Shreveport, Louisiana, is the home of the Azaleas. As spring begins, people travel miles to admire this bush, so brilliant and full of color. In Shreveport, the splendor of an Azalea can be found in the courtyards of the most affluent neighborhood homes and in the yard of a two-room shack. For a short time each spring, vivid Azaleas blanket the city with a beauty that belies the barriers of class, race, and economics that separate. And then they're gone, just as quickly as they came. You wake up one morning and the once vibrant flowers are dull and lifeless.

    My experiences as a police officer influence my way of looking at Azaleas. The enthusiastic generosity with which they share their beauty reminds me of the innocence of a little girl, the fresh beauty of a young woman, the love of a mother, the devotion of a wife, and the trust of an elderly woman. The speed of their passing recalls the suddenness with which I have seen the innocence, beauty, love, devotion, and trust of these women and their families shattered by a violent act.

I'm not saying that women should not be innocent, beautiful, loving, devoted, and trusting. We appreciate the beauty of the Azalea all the more because we know that it is fragile. Women should be aware of their surroundings, practical in their dealings with others, and empowered to protect themselves and their children. That is why I wrote this book on violent crimes against women and children. I hope to protect the women and children who remain—to spare a family the bereavement and burden that others have had to endure.

Also, I wrote this book as a wake-up call for women and girls. We must be mentally alert and learn from the experiences of others so our fragile existence is never shattered by senseless violence.

Introduction

Many citizens will never face the prospect of viewing the body of a victim of violent crime. Police officers encounter such sights often. In my ten years as a police officer, I have learned to endure these moments, but I am not immune to the pain and damage such acts inflict on the victims as well as their loved ones and the communities in which they occur.

Violent crimes against women and their children are particularly troubling since the victims are typically innocent of having instigated the attack. I've often wondered if some of the deaths of women and children could have been prevented. I've often thought to myself, if only she could have done this or if she had known that, maybe she would be here still.

I think this especially when family members show up at a crime scene where a loved one has been murdered. Children and husbands scream out inconsolably for their loved one, and they cannot be appeased because death is final. Death is irreversible. A mom, daughter, or sister is not coming back. Their loved one no longer lives. Their shared plans and dreams are just that—dreams.

Violence against women includes threatening or actual use of physical, psychological, or sexual abuse. The most common referenced behaviors include homicide, domestic violence, partner abuse, psychological abuse, same sex violence, women battering, date violence, spousal abuse, elder abuse, sexual assault, courtship violence, date rape, acquaintance rape, and marital and stranger rape. Growing up in a cycle of violence and abuse with a distorted concept of manhood are root causes of violence. Statistics vary because reporting procedures vary from state to state. Violence against women can begin early as child abuse, and while some women are never directly abused, others encounter multiple forms of abuse. Some additional root causes of violence include, but are not limited to:

- Poverty and unemployment
- Hopelessness and despair
- Alcohol and substance abuse
- Underemployment and economic disequilibrium
- Circumstances of racism and injustice

Women whose lifestyles don't reflect these characteristics are nevertheless likely to become victims of violence and should not take these issues lightly.

Though the most common form of abuse against elderly women is maltreatment, instances of physical abuse, exploitation, emotional abuse, and sexual abuse are increasing. The most common victims of elder abuse are women with chronic illness or disability. In most cases the perpetrator is an adult child, other family member, or spouse. This fact can lull elderly women into thinking that strangers can be trusted, especially if they are polite or polished. Don't let your defenses down for anything or anyone. It's not worth the risk.
Women with a history of sexual abuse are also at increased risk for unintended pregnancy, sexually transmitted infections, and adverse pregnancy outcomes. Yet, victims of violence who seek care from health professionals often do not have providers who recognize, ask about, or know how to address these needs. Providers can reassure women that violence is unacceptable. No woman deserves to be beaten, sexually abused, or made to suffer emotionally. Health professionals should also give empathy and support by

providing medical treatments, offering counseling, documenting injuries, and referring their clients to legal assistance and support services.

If you think that violence against women ends with the violent act, you are wrong. Children who grow up in homes where they observe violence are four times more likely than others to be violent when they grow up. The cycle of violence perpetuates itself. In order for us to get along well in this world, we must keep our eyes and ears open. We must hear and observe and be able to act. We must realize that true observation studies experience and draws conclusions from it. Women should not stand idly by and allow things to happen to them. We must fight and face the responsibility of protecting our children, even if it means sacrificing a comfortable lifestyle. It will pay a tremendous reward in the long run.

The stories you are about to read are true. However, the names and a few photos have been altered to protect the victims. I recommend you pass this book on to your teenage daughters, moms, sisters, and perhaps your sons as well. Some stories are very graphic and descriptive. They are too graphic for the extremely young, but hopefully just graphic enough to awaken women to what is going on in the real world, thereby saving lives.

Chapter 1

I'm Too Young

    I often reminisce—in wonder—about those youthful days not long ago. I was young and nonchalant. Only by the grace of God did I escape the darkness of destruction. We often feel indestructible. We can't imagine anything bad happening to us. Why should we? We are young, attractive, and have few responsibilities. The Azaleas are colorful. Life is great! Ladies, keep it that way while you can.

    First Peter 5:8 says, "Be sober, be vigilant; because your adversary the devil walks about like a roaring lion, seeking whom he may devour." Jesus said we are to "be wise as serpents and harmless as doves" (Matthew 10:16).

    If you have your own apartment, be cautious not to advertise your single lifestyle. It doesn't take much for someone to map your everyday routine. Be watchful and conscientious.

Dianna Cook Thomas

Jean's Story

    As Jean walked back and forth through her apartment complex with her laundry, she was tracked by a subject. She'd traveled that path hundreds of times and never thought of danger. She was unaware of being followed because her pursuer blended in as a normal everyday kind of guy. Besides, the complex was in a safe middle-class environment.
    As Jean walked toward her apartment, the subject appeared out of nowhere and forced her into a vacant unit. He held his hand over her mouth and dared her to scream. The vacant apartment was dark. He tore off her clothes and sexually assaulted her. If she screamed, he had threatened to kill her. She was afraid of what was to come, but there was no way to prevent it. He raped and sodomized her. She had to obey his every command. She felt disgraced, dirty, and terrified. She also thought if she gave him what he wanted, he would let her go.
    Men who have spent any length of time in prison have learned never to leave any witnesses. That's why it's so important to be careful before getting caught in their web. Jean's thoughts were wrong. He didn't let her go. The only sure way of not being caught was to exterminate his witness. He stabbed her twice in the chest, breaking the knife off inside of her.
    She couldn't believe it was happening to her. At one point she thought she was only dreaming and she would do things differently when she woke up. She would be more careful wherever she went. She'd always make sure to do her laundry with several friends.
    Jean began to lose consciousness, and the perpetrator thought she was dead, but she wasn't. She lay in the cold, empty room for twelve hours and awoke feeling isolated and baffled. She summoned all of her strength and crawled to a nearby apartment to seek help. Everyone at the complex became more careful and they began to walk around in groups, even to do laundry.
    But the damage had already been done to Jean. The perpetrator was never located and her life will never be the same, especially with her attacker still out there looking for someone else to harm.
    Adjusting to a new life wasn't easy for Jean, but as time went on she realized because of this traumatic

experience that life can be good if you practice safety and wisdom.

Jean didn't know her attacker, but many women do know their abuser. It's often a husband or a lover. Many cases of domestic violence often culminate with the victim's death, and many cases of assault often leaves the victim wishing they were dead.

A Familiar Face

Most domestic cases proceed like this: Mom and Dad get into an argument, Mom abuses Dad or Dad abuses Mom. Correct? Not so in this dispute.

In this particular case, a mom was married for the second time. She had two teenage daughters from her first marriage. The stepdad was employed, but the stress of his job became overwhelming. He went to work with a smile on his face and came home in a rage. Tension mounted each day and things were building to a climax.

The situation reached its peak when the stepdad lost his job. He was tired and disgusted with no way to support his family. He came home that day disheartened and despondent. The weight of the world was on his shoulders. As if being fired wasn't bad enough, his wife began to demand answers to several questions about the loss of his job. These questions escalated to, "How are the bills going to be paid?" An argument ensued, and they began quarreling fiercely. Matters turned violent. The stepdad and mom struggled, then the stepdad pulled out a knife and stabbed his wife. The two teenage daughters, who had frequently been told to stay out of their parents' affairs, heard Mom screaming and jumped up to see what was going on. Discovering that the stepdad was stabbing their mom, they naturally jumped in to defend her. He stabbed them as well. He vacated the scene as neighbors notified the police.

All three victims were rushed to the hospital. The mother and her oldest teen survived, but the fifteen-year-old died. This mother will never forgive herself for the loss of her blameless child. She questions herself daily, wondering what she could have done differently—like leave the violent marriage years earlier.

Dianna Cook Thomas

Escalating Violence

    The intensity of domestic violence is escalating. It seems that when families had fewer material belongings, they were better able to appreciate each other's company and cherish their moments together. Now we have brick homes, new cars, money, VCRs, TVs, and a myriad of other luxuries, but we can't get along with each other. Children die at the hands of a parent or stepparent because they are caught up in a domestic dispute. Domestic violence has existed since I can remember, but in my youth there were fewer instances of fatal abuse.

    Increased expectations are part of the problem. We live in a consumer society where acquisition of material possessions is viewed as success. People feel pressured to acquire the right possessions to project an image of success, even if they have to put themselves deeply in debt to do it. No wonder people get depressed. Acquisition of wealth is not a sound basis for building self-esteem. Stress caused by financial worries fosters short tempers and explosive situations.

    Children feel these pressures perhaps even more strongly than their parents. Adolescents feel a tremendous need to "fit in." In our society that means having the right possessions. Depression in the younger generation often leads to addictions and suicide.

    Throughout life there will always be difficult moments. Ask your grandparents. Nothing, absolutely nothing, is worth taking your life over. Not a boyfriend, girlfriend, husband, wife, a traumatic experience, a job, absolutely nothing. People have endured far worse experiences than any of your worst encounters, yet they have lived to tell about it. Of course, they may choose not to talk about it—that's their choice—but they have still endured. Try to pattern your life after someone who is positive, not the town freak or your local drug dealer—who, no doubt, has plenty of cash and all of the "right" things.

Proverbs 4:5-7 says:

"Get wisdom! Get understanding! Do not forget, nor turn away from the words of my mouth.
Do not forsake her, and she will preserve you; love her, and she will keep you.
Wisdom is the principal thing; therefore get wisdom. And in all your getting, get understanding."

Verses 10-13 of this same chapter say:

"Hear, my son, and receive my sayings, and the years of your life will be many.
I have taught you in the way of wisdom; I have led you in right paths.
When you walk, your steps will not be hindered, and when you run, you will not stumble.
Take firm hold of instruction, do not let go; keep her, for she is your life."

Hopeless

I made a call once on a twenty-year-old who was very depressed and threatening suicide. As I drove up to the house, I couldn't help but notice how small it was. It was a four-room shack, with one window unit air conditioner. It was a hot July. The single Azalea bush in the front yard had long ago lost its blooms. It waited in the heat, knowing that another spring would come, bringing with it new hope.
I knocked on the door. A young girl around the age of seven answered and let me in. The mother was in another room without air-conditioning or even a fan to cool the heat. I asked what her problem was. She told me that she had five children, was jobless, and had no one to turn to. She wanted to kill herself.
I asked the whereabouts of the other children, and she told me they were in the other room. I went to check on them, and as I lifted an old, dirty curtain for a door, I saw the five children watching television. I spoke. They spoke. No one smiled. There was no glee or laughter in their hearts. I went back to the mother and tried to advise her spiritually. As we talked, I

finally got to the root of her problem. Not only did she have five children ages seven, five, four, two, and one, but she was now pregnant by a married man. All of this by the young age of twenty.

When this married man, whom she had loved with all her heart, discovered she was pregnant, he told her he didn't care for her or "that damn baby." He broke off the fling they were having. She was left alone and depressed. It seems she spent the last few days with hope and disappointment chasing each other in an endless loop through her mind.

The psalmist David said to the Lord, "My hope is in You" (Psalm 39:7). In Jeremiah 17:7, Jeremiah spoke a word from the Lord: "Blessed is the man who trusts in the Lord, and whose hope is the Lord."

You see, instead of allowing her energy to go toward loving and caring for her children, she wasted her love on a married man. She could not see that a better life could not develop from this bad situation. She needed to direct her love upward to God and inward toward herself and her family, not outward toward a man. Affairs are never the answer to raising your children to be sound and stable. Married men have no interest in raising your children. They have children of their own to raise.

I advised her after she had the new baby, her love should go to her children and she should place the love of a companion on the back burner until she was better established financially. If she thought that a failed affair was heartbreaking, how would she respond when her children went astray? That is a nightmare within itself. If a woman spends all of her time loving her lover, who will love her children?

Sometimes the best of plans do go awry. Changing circumstances demand that we adapt to them. If your ship doesn't come in on schedule, adjust to the disappointment. It will arrive eventually if you hold a steady course. It will not be easy for this young woman to raise six children by herself, but it can happen. My grandmother raised nine by herself after my granddad left her, and it made her the dynamic lady that she is today.

No Other Friend

What really amazes me is that God, the Creator of the universe, the great I AM, the One who was, is, and is to come, seeks the company of you and me. Given who He is and who we are, I can only shake my head in wonder and breathe a prayer of thanks that He considers us worth wooing, worth loving, worth the death of His precious Son. And all He asks of us is to let Him be a friend who is closer than a brother instead of simply a casual acquaintance. "There is a friend who sticks closer than a brother" (Proverbs 18:24). That's Jesus!

When I learned to seek Him in times of despair or discouragement and let Him be this friend, I found that no matter what my sin, He still calls me friend. No matter how crimson the stain of sin, He can wash our hearts whiter than snow.

To start this young woman on the right path and because she was so weak, I called her relatives so she could be committed to an institution and receive counseling. I had to be that friend who would lay it all out for her and tell it to her straight.

I continued to tell her nothing is worth taking your life over. Six children can be a blessing. Let's face it. They were there and she couldn't put them back. If you cannot or will not love and take care of them, someone else will! There is no acceptable reason to mistreat or neglect your children. Don't look at them as a means of retaliation against someone else.

I used to wonder when I saw a woman who was in an abusive relationship, "Why doesn't she just quit him or leave?" I suppose it is one of the most frequently asked questions about domestic violence and abuse. There are a number of reasons why victims remain in abusive relationships.

Hope - Many women love their abusive partners and hope things will improve. They look back to better times in the relationship and believe that things can get back to "the way they used to be." Abusers often treat their victims very well during the honeymoon phase that follows a violent episode, and this encourages the victim to believe that things will improve.

Fear - Abusers often threaten to hurt or kill the victim if she leaves.

Social Pressure - Our society places a high value on having a partner, and many women believe it is better to have an abusive partner than none at all. Well-meaning friends and family may even discourage a victim from leaving an abuser for this reason.

Low Self-Esteem - Women in violent relationships often question themselves. They may blame themselves for their abuser's behavior, and the abuser habitually reinforces this feeling. Constant humiliation eats away at the victim's self-confidence, thus she may come to believe that she is totally helpless. In long-term relationships, these factors may also influence a victim to remain in an abusive situation.

Isolation - The abuser often criticizes or behaves badly toward the victim's friends and family, making it difficult for the victim to maintain any relationships other than her relationship with the abuser.

Financial Dependence - The victim may believe that she cannot support herself and her children without the abusive partner's help. Also, abusers routinely control access to money and forbid victims to hold a job or get job training.

Domestic violence is a crime. It occurs among all races, ages, and religions. It happens to people of all educational and income levels. Remember, an incident is rarely an isolated occurrence. Abuse usually recurs frequently and escalates in severity over time.

In some cases, batterers are life endangering. It is possible to evaluate whether they are likely to kill their partners, children, family members, or others. Here are some additional tips to be able to help assess whether batterers will kill:

Pet Abuse - Those who assault and mutilate pets are more likely to kill a close family member.

Weapons - When a batterer possesses weapons and has used or threatened to use them in the past in his assaults on the battered woman, the children, or himself, access to those weapons increases his potential for lethal assault.

Fantasies of Homicide or Suicide - The more detailed a batterer's fantasy about whom, how, when, and/or where to kill, the more treacherous he is. The batterer who has previously acted out part of a homicide or suicide fantasy may be invested in killing as a viable "solution" to his problems.

Rage - The most life-endangering rage often erupts when a batterer believes the battered woman is leaving him.

Obsessiveness About Partner or Family - A man who is obsessive about his female partner, who either idolizes her and feels that he cannot live without her or believes he is entitled to her no matter what because she is his wife, is more likely to be life endangering.

Depression - Where a batterer has been acutely depressed and sees little hope for moving beyond the depression, he may be a candidate for homicide or suicide.

Threats of Homicide or Suicide - The batterer who has threatened to kill himself, his partner, their children, or her relatives must be considered extremely dangerous.

Drug or Alcohol Consumption - Consumption of drugs or alcohol when in a state of despair or fury can elevate risk of lethality.

Profile of an Abuser

Here are some indicators of lethality in the lifestyle of an abuser:

- Prior use of a deadly weapon
- Hostage taking
- Separation from the victim or termination of the relationship
- Suicide attempts
- Escalating frequency and severity of violence
- Violence towards children
- Public violence
- Sexual abuse
- Threats to kill
- Alcohol or drug abuse
- Stalking
- Obsessive jealousy

Ask yourself, does the person you love...

- Blame his outbursts and anger on you?
- Call you hurtful names?
- Keep track of your time and seem possessive?
- Destroy personal property?
- Hit, punch, slap, kick, or threaten to hurt you or your children?
- Accuse you of infidelity?
- Control all finances/force you to account for your spending in detail?
- Humiliate you in front of others?
- Use or threaten to use a weapon against you?
- Keep you from working or going to school?
- Expect you to be perfect and have all household chores done and dinner ready, or else?
- Discourage relationships with family and friends?
- Get easily insulted?

Child Abuse

Batterers of women very often engage in child abuse as well, though they do not account for all instances of child abuse. Child abuse is any mistreatment or neglect of a child that results in non-accidental harm or injury which cannot be reasonably explained. This may include physical abuse, emotional abuse, sexual abuse, and neglect.

The number of abused or neglected children is steadily increasing. In one year alone, authorities received three million reports involving the maltreatment of approximately four million children. The most common form of child maltreatment is neglect. Physical abuse is the next highest, followed by sexual abuse, emotional abuse, and medical neglect.

It is often difficult to determine whether injury to a child is accidental or intentional. The next scenario illustrates this fact. You be the judge. Cyndra and Malcolm were a young married couple who had two children ages fifteen months and three years. Caring for two children this young is a challenge requiring much love and patience. Young parents like Cyndra and Malcolm often find themselves without the maturity and emotional reserves necessary for such a task.

I Can't See the Azaleas
True Crimes Against Women and Children

    This marriage was showing signs of failure. Malcolm often left when quarrels started, leaving Cyndra alone to care for the active toddlers. One sunny day in June, the couple had a disagreement. One thing led to another and Malcolm left the house, slamming the door behind him. Then a not-so-unusual event happened at the worst possible moment. The fifteen-month-old wet his diaper.
    Frustrated, Cyndra began to run a tub of bath water. She sat the child in the water and left the room to put a load of towels in the washer. She went back to check on the baby and he told her, "Mommy, hot." She reached into the tub to check the water, ran cold water to cool it down, and then turned the hot water back on to warm it up again. That's when he began crying.
    Cyndra stated that she took him out of the water. When Malcolm returned home, he saw that the child was in agony and asked her what was wrong with the baby. She didn't answer his question, but she started to yell at him. So he gathered the children up and took the baby to the hospital. Detective Suzanne was called out by the hospital staff. This is mandatory when a child's injury does not match up with the parent's explanation of how it happened.
    Detective Suzanne questioned both parents. Because Malcolm was not in the home when the incident occurred, he was eliminated as a possible suspect. That left Cyndra as the main suspect in this child abuse case. Cyndra's statements were conflicting and her attitude toward her son's injuries was nonchalant. An argument ensued between Detective Suzanne and Cyndra about the injuries caused by Cyndra's seemingly gross negligence.
    Detective Suzanne is a kind person, caring and giving. She will take an abused child into her home in a heartbeat. However, she can also be hard-nosed, tough, and firm. She has zero tolerance for individuals who abuse those who can't care for themselves. She is a one-woman army against abuse and neglect with an eye for even the most minute detail.
    The detective decided to go out to the family home since there was no other way of knowing the accurate temperature of the water in the home. She turned on the water in the bathtub and placed her hand under it as it flowed from the spout. After ten seconds, the water began running hot and forced the detective to immediately remove her hand. She could not leave her hand under the running water even for a second.

Dianna Cook Thomas

This angered Detective Suzanne, for she could only think of how the toddler had suffered for the minutes he had stood in the water. He stood there long enough to suffer second- and third-degree burns. The following photos show a nurse holding the left leg of the toddler. There's a large pool of fluid around the ankle and foot, making the foot appear to be four times its normal size. The rest of the child's foot is wrapped in a sterile bandage that had to be redressed frequently. The right leg had an accumulation of fluid encompassing its entire lower portion.

Detective Suzanne explained to me that this type of burn in toddlers is known as "Stocking Burns." A Stocking Burn is a burn to the hand or feet usually caused by intentional immersion. The burn has the appearance of a stocking or a glove on the feet or hands because the child tries to brace against being forced farther into the hot water. There may also be burns on the buttocks from the caregiver trying to force the child to sit in scalding water.

The evidence just didn't match Cyndra's story. Her story would have produced evidence of burns over the entire lower body from above the waist to the toes. She was arrested and transported to jail.

A great number of children die from child abuse injuries inflicted as unreasonable, severe corporal punishment, or unjustifiable punishment. This usually happens when a frustrated or angry parent strikes, shakes, or throws a child. Physical abuse injuries result from punching, beating, kicking, biting, burning, or otherwise harming a child. While any of these injuries can occur accidentally when a child is at play, physical abuse should be suspected if the explanations do not fit the injury or if a pattern of frequency is apparent. The longer the abuse continues, the more serious the injuries to the child, and the more difficult it is to eliminate the abusive behavior.

I Can't See the Azaleas
True Crimes Against Women and Children

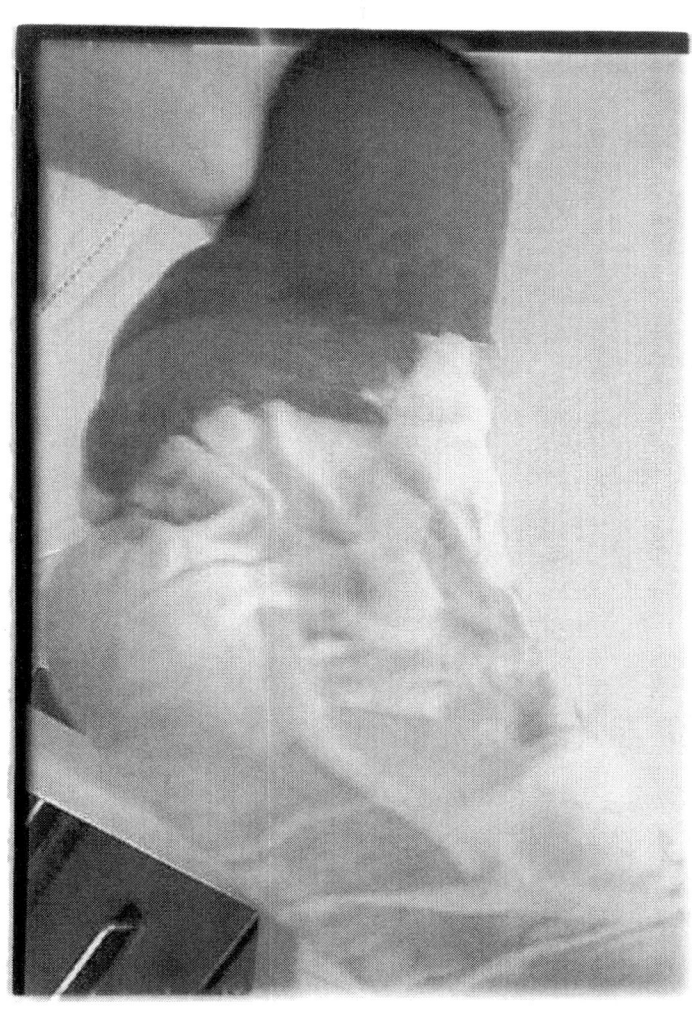

The nurse is holding the leg of a child where the discharge is very pronounced.

Dianna Cook Thomas

What makes people abuse children? Sometimes it could be that the parent is simply unaware of the magnitude of force with which he or she strikes a child. Most parents want to be good parents, but sometimes lose control and are unable to cope. Some factors which contribute to child abuse include:

- Immaturity of parents
- Lack of parenting skills
- Unrealistic expectations about children's behavior and capabilities
- A parent's own negative childhood experiences
- Social isolation
- Frequent family crises
- Drug or alcohol problems

There are many warning signs, though one or two isolated incidents do not necessarily indicate criminal abuse. Keep watching until you are reasonably sure, and then report suspected abuse to the authorities. Look for the following:

Physical abuse - Sores, burns, or bruises on the body. Reluctance or vagueness in describing how injuries originated. Bruises and burns are the most persistent physical symptoms.

Sexual abuse - Precocious behavior; sexual knowledge displayed through language or behavior that is beyond what is normal for a child's age; copying adult sexual behavior, inappropriate sexual behavior such as kissing on the mouth and/or attempting to insert the tongue in your mouth; soreness, redness, chaffing around the genitals; inappropriate sexual play with other children, themselves, toys, or pets.

Neglect - Soiled diapers, dirty hair, unwashed clothes, and body odor.

Emotional or mental abuse - This type of abuse is particularly difficult to determine because some children are normally quiet, which can also be a sign of emotional abuse. Lack of self-esteem is another symptom, but again, that does not mean children are abused.

Child abuse is a sign that parents are having difficulty coping with their situation. Parents need to realize, among other things, that being abused or neglected as a child increases the likelihood of arrest when the child matures.

Chapter 2

I'm Too Pretty

To be considered pretty is a blessing and a compliment. As women, we seek ways to look more appealing, and we spend billions of dollars to attain that goal. We expect men to appreciate and admire our appearance. But, ladies, sick-minded people admire beauty as well. They may even track you.

On a bright and sunny day, clouds like cotton, birds chirping the melody of a blissful love song, everything was going well for a winsome young girl living in a suburban area. She had everything to live for. She may have wanted one day to be Miss America or to fall in love with a handsome prince with a promising future. Perhaps she wanted a successful career traveling abroad and to have children who would look just like herself and her prince.

She was well aware of the beauty of the Azalea blossom. But she refused to acknowledge its impermanence. All of her possibilities came to a halt when someone broke into her apartment. The access was so easy because there were no dead bolts, just glass panes near the door knob. She was caught off guard, never realizing that harm can come to pretty girls. She was slightly self-centered, as the pretty sometimes are, and thought the world revolved around her. She felt nothing could happen to her because she was pretty, and people like pretty girls—but she was wrong.

When the police found this pretty girl, she was sitting up in her bed with her back against the headboard. There was thick semen dripping from her mouth and onto her exposed breast. A broomstick handle had been rammed three-and-a-half inches into her vagina. Her last minutes in life were spent in a cheapening and perverted manner. Screaming was in vain because there was no one to hear her frantic cries. There was no one to come to her aid. Her last few minutes alive were spent satisfying the perversions of her attacker.

Violent crime happens to pretty girls just like it happens to anyone else. Pretty girls are never untouchable to a criminal. Understand that pretty to a certain type of criminal mind is an invitation to harm in an abhorrent way. The glass pane door should not be in the home of a single lady. Be safe and secure always. When leaving and entering your home, make sure you are escorted by a male friend if possible. When entering, check to see if anything is out of place. If so, leave immediately and call the police. Take responsibility for your own safety. Absolutely no one can take care of you but you. Keep your doors locked at all times. Always know your surroundings before and after you enter your home. Place additional locks on your front and back doors.

Guard Your Steps

Don't be caught off guard like another pretty young girl who should have had a long life ahead of her. An unknown individual admired her beauty as he quietly stalked her goings and comings. One day the chance finally arrived for him to catch her in a vulnerable situation. He made his way inside her apartment and began to hit her in the head with a hammer. Afterwards, he stuck a syringe, filled with acid, into her neck. Then he tried to choke her.

She was a struggler and continued to fight back, but the killer wasn't finished. He stabbed her repeatedly with two kitchen knives. She started to gasp for air and relief. She tried to play dead, but he stomped her pretty face and stomach as she lay on the floor. And if that weren't good enough, as she wondered when it would all be over, he put her in the back of his truck and drove her to a remote location. She probably thought he was going to rape her. Instead, he dragged her out of the truck and left her there, dropping a large log he had found in the woods, onto her head. As he turned his vehicle around to leave, he ran over her several times. Her lifeless body was found by a passerby.

Not a pretty site for a pretty girl. But who would do such a horrible thing to a resplendent beauty? What motive could there be? Monsters do not need a motive.

Perpetrators such as these don't care about your drop dead gorgeous looks or your appealing beauty. Let your conscience be informed by reality. In Ecclesiastes 8:2,5 Solomon said, "'Keep the king's commandment for the sake of your oath to God'...He who keeps his command will experience nothing harmful; and a wise man's heart discerns both time and judgment." In Hebrews, chapter 5, where the author talks about milk and the solid food or meat of the Word, or spiritual maturity, he says:

> "For everyone who partakes only of milk is unskilled in the word of righteousness, for he is a babe.
> But solid food belongs to those who are of full age, that is, those who by reason of use have their senses exercised to discern both good and evil."

Verses 13, 14

The act of discerning and admitting to yourself that there are people out there who will kill you, will allow you to keep yourself out of compromising situations. Without this recognition, you will blunder.

Your natural intuition as well as the Holy Spirit give off caution signs and a forewarning from within. Jesus said, "However, when He, the Spirit of truth, has come, He will guide you into all truth..." (John 16:13). Either we acknowledge these caution signs and warnings, perhaps feeling a little moronic because it turns out we are wrong (but still unharmed and alive), or we choose to ignore them because we're afraid our caution will make us look silly. Carelessness can look silly, too, especially when it leads to death. Women may not realize that they are being stalked, but vigilance may thwart a stalker's plans.

Why do violent crimes happen to undeserving victims? Sometimes it can be our own bad choices and sometimes not. Sometimes women may say to themselves, "I want to do what I want to do." Yes, you have the right to choose your path, but consider the consequences before deciding.

It is true, women have died doing the right thing. The victim of a violent, unprovoked crime is never to blame for the attack, no matter how careless her actions. But that doesn't mean you shouldn't try to make yourself a less likely target for criminals and predators. Actions have consequences, and considering them may save your life. Please learn from those whose lives have ended tragically. Relish life while you're young and pretty, but use common sense while doing so.

Attackers often consider cell phones a distraction technique. Predators watch for women who are chattering away on their cell phones, completely unaware of their surroundings. Always glance around while conversing on the phone. Give 75 percent of your attention to your surroundings and 25 percent to the person on the phone. The person on the phone can't step in and help you if you're attacked. He or she can only notify the police who will try to figure out where you were last. Also, look in the reflection of a window to see what's behind you when you're shopping or walking up to your house or a building.

Listen for sounds behind you, turn around and see who's approaching. The most opportune time for evading an attack is when the suspect is approaching you. That is when you will have time to make counter moves or scream loudly in a high-pitched tone. If you're overtaken while you are preoccupied on the cell phone or distracted in some other way, there is very little time to act.

A criminal's first intention is to catch you off guard—the element of surprise. Then he has time to contemplate his next maneuver. By surprising you, he has a victim who is inattentive with no preplanned counter moves. Sometimes he may figure that you are off guard, but instead you are ready to counteract. He is bewildered because you have a plan. This catches him off guard.

Valuable Lesson

Learn from the woman who was assaulted in 2001 by someone trying to steal her car from the parking lot of a local grocery store. As she approached her vehicle, an intruder attacked her from behind. She fought back with all her might by beating on him. He never thought that a woman would have the strength or the audacity to do that. As she began to whip him, probably out of embarrassment or retaliation, he shot her. Luckily she was not seriously injured.

She had a plan, but she made numerous mistakes in the execution of it. Sometimes fighting back only makes a perpetrator more violent. This one had a gun. Don't assume that an attacker doesn't have a weapon—most do. Never fight a person with a gun. Let them have whatever they want, whether it's the car or the purse. The suspect only wanted her car. If he'd wanted her, he would have thrown her into the car immediately. Her first thought and plan should have been to get away from him as quickly as possible and to do so without being harmed.

In the summer of 1991, two young and pretty girls went to a club one night to dance the evening away. One girl, Amy, twenty-one years old, had a little more to drink than she should have, and the other, Neenah, twenty, had a few drinks but was fairly clearheaded. They danced with various guys that night and had a fun time. Soon after the club closed, the girls headed to their car.

Two guys, known as suspect number one and suspect number two, asked them for a ride home. Amy, the owner of the car, said, "Yes." Neenah said, "Absolutely not!" They argued about it—these two men were total strangers and both were very massive guys. Neenah insisted, "Don't." Amy overruled her. Amy asked them if they had any guns, and suspect number one held his arm out and stated, "What! Do I look like I have a gun to you?" Amy said, "No, you seem like a real nice guy and everything."

Neenah was so afraid she almost freaked out. Both men sat in the backseat of the car. Neenah thought to herself, I swear to God, I'm going to kill Amy when we drop these fellows off. How could she do something so stupid? She wondered if they could really trust them. Maybe it would turn out all right. After all, she and Amy were too pretty for anything to happen to them!

Then one guy said, "Pull over. Here it is." Then he put his hand over Amy's mouth and put a gun to her head. While she was mumbling he said, "Shut up, Bitch."

Neenah jumped out and ran. Suspect number two jumped out, caught her, and hit her in the face with his gun. Neenah fell to the ground, losing teeth in the process.

As the blood washed down Neenah's face, she pleaded, "Please don't kill me! Please don't rape me. I'm a virgin."

Her attacker laughed and said, "That's a lie if I've ever heard one. There are no twenty-year-old virgins. What kind of game are you playing?"

He then pulled down her pants and started to rape her. He smelled deplorable. Next, he wanted her to masturbate him with her hands. Then it was oral and anal sex, over and over again. The mere thought of these acts would have made her sick. Now she was being forced to perform them.

Neenah tried to run again, and her attacker caught her. Again, he struck her, knocking out a couple more of her teeth. Other teeth were dislodged as well. Her lip was split, and blood was all over her face and body. Not only that, she now smelled like him.

Neenah became completely distraught and begged, "Just go on and kill me. I can't take any more of this. After this I'm going to kill myself anyway." By now she was tired, dirty, frightened, and had semen all over her face and body. He took her head and shoved it in the ground with all the strength he had.

Then he stopped. Amy was still in the car with suspect number one, being raped and sodomized. Amy's attacker had taken all of her money and jewelry, but that wasn't important, to say the least.

Amy pleaded with suspect number one, "Please just let us go. You got what you wanted."

His reply, "We ain't through with you yet."

Neenah and suspect number two returned to the car. Neenah tried to button up her torn blouse, but she had no buttons because all of them had been popped off. So she had to use her hands and arms to cover herself.

While they were all back in the car, the young women pleaded, "Please don't do anything to us. We won't tell anyone."

Suspect number one told Neenah, "I don't like you, Bitch. You scream too much. I'm gonna kill you first."

They were forced to drive to another location, a more secluded and dark place. They spent three-and-a-half hours there being raped repeatedly by each suspect, sometimes in front of each other. They had to drive to another location which was a vacant house. This house was shabby and disgusting. The girls were subjected to rape and sodomy. They could only think of the wrong choice they made back at the nightclub. What could they have done differently to spare them from the misery that they were encountering at present?

Ultimately, they were placed in the trunk of the car. They presumed they would be thrown over a cliff or left there to die. They moaned and whispered to each other. Their hearts were pounding. Finally, the car stopped. The trunk opened, and they were ordered to get out. They were coerced to walk a short distance but could scarcely see because there were no lights, just wildernesses and dark sky. Both were frightened, whimpering, and hurting. Their eyes, noses, and mouths were bleeding and swollen. They could barely walk because of the contorted positions they had been forced into. Suddenly, shots fired. Neenah could hear them as clear as a bell. She could feel the warm blood running down her body. She moaned, "It hurts so bad." Then she fell.

More shots were fired. Amy fell. The suspects took off in Amy's car only to return and shoot both of them one more time. Neenah said that they put the gun to her head and she heard a "Pow." Oh, how it hurts, she thought. Then she heard another "Pow." Neenah glanced at Amy. She was barely moving. Neenah knew that no matter how bad she was hurting she had to seek help.

They were in mud and weeds. Neenah asked, "Can you hear me, Amy?" Amy mumbled. Neenah whispered, "I love you, Amy."

They were in so much pain, and Neenah could hear Amy whimpering. The suspects came back again. Neenah and Amy lay still, playing dead. The attackers left, but Neenah couldn't know if they would be coming back. She had to make her move. She left Amy as she slowly got up and left to get help.

Dianna Cook Thomas

Blood was running down Neenah's stomach and legs as well as from her head. As she ran through the dark night trying to find a road, she kept falling to the ground. She was half naked with her private parts exposed. She had to find help, but feared that she would run upon the suspects instead of rescuers. Her heart pounded and she trembled. She kept going, her heart pounding harder and harder.

Eventually, someone saw her and stopped, but was horrified by her appearance and drove off. About five minutes later, the same vehicle came back with two people in it. "But what if it's them again? Or another maniac?" she feared. Fortunately, two city workers had found her. They took her to the local Fire Department and called the police.

Neenah survived this ordeal because of her strong will to live. Amy wasn't so lucky. She died in the wilderness, alone. It was Neenah's first time to ever go to that club and her last.

Investigators were called out to the hospital. They exhausted all of that night and the following day investigating this crime, fearing that the perpetrators might strike again, but most of all wanting someone to pay for their violent, inhumane actions against two innocent victims. They fingerprinted the crime scene of the vacant house. They got the license plate number from Neenah, and the detectives gave a broadcast to all units. The car was later found near the first crime scene. This gave investigators more evidence and fingerprints. After extensive investigation, the two suspects were caught. Police were able to match their fingerprints because both had prior records. Suspect number one had just gotten out of the penitentiary less than a week before the attack.

Girls, do you see how mindless this is? One or two drinks or a little bit of drugs can make Dracula look like Denzel. It'll make Sylvester the cat, look like Stone Phillips. It'll make a creature look like Tom Cruse. Looks can be tempting, but I advise you to beware.

Listen to your inner feelings and those of your friends when they tell you, "No, something is not right," or, "No, don't do it." Neenah's life has been changed forever, and Amy's life is over. No stranger needs a ride home. If he made it to the club, he'll make it back just fine. They can curse you out and call

I Can't See the Azaleas
True Crimes Against Women and Children

you a bitch, but that's okay. You will be just fine at home, safe and asleep in your bed.

Chapter 3

I'm Too Ugly

When has being unattractive ever mattered to a maniac? As a matter of fact, women who have low self-esteem are easy targets for predators. These women often overlook the warning signs that should tell them to stay away because they are desperate to be accepted. It's better to be single and alive than to have been brutally beaten or killed by a man whom you let in your life so you wouldn't be alone. Don't let low self-esteem get you killed or severely wounded. And besides, who decides who's pretty and who's not?

Have you ever noticed that your perception of a person's "beauty" changes as you get to know him or her? The beauty of a "pretty" girl may disappear once you get to know her. She may be the type of person referred to in the old saying, "He who finds no fault in himself may need a second opinion." Conversely, we've all met women who seemed unremarkable at first, only to grow increasingly aware of their beauty as we become friends.

I used to wear a lot of makeup to try to brighten up my face. My husband told me, "You look so much better without makeup." I trusted his judgment, especially in the beginning of our marriage. So I stopped wearing some of it. Sorry hubby, can't do without my lipstick! Don't ever think you're so ugly that an amiable man wouldn't come near you or find you appealing.

I've seen all types of dead bodies. Young, old, small, large, black, white, brown, yellow, attractive, unattractive. They all have one thing in common; they are dead. They can't change a thing. They can't undo problems or come up with an answer to a simple one. All problems have an answer. It's whether one can choose the right one that matters. Stay strong and fight to live.

I have a relative who is what one would call unattractive. Yet, she's cheerful and she takes care of herself. She has lived to be an old lady and still has an intuitive sense for danger. Late one night, a prowler was outside her house. She can't hear very well, but she can see a spider pee a hundred miles away, or as my grandma would say, "She could see a gnat's ass in Georgia."

Looking between the curtains of her living room window, she saw the suspect. She grabbed her pistol, jumped onto the couch, landing on her stomach, head toward the window. She held the gun securely with both hands, cocking the trigger back with one thumb. Her legs were bent at the knees with her feet crossed in the air. Her eyes were aligned with the sites on her gun, and she yelled to the perpetrator, "You brang yo ass in here if you wont to. I got somethin' fa you!"

The prowler left, speedily. She told the police she would have killed him dead if he had stepped one foot through her window! And she meant it!

One should be alert and ready to take action when confronted with an unknown situation. Don't wait until it's too late to make a plan. This prowler never made it past the window. I'm also sure word got out to other criminals that this lady will take action, "And she ain't scared either."

Looks Aren't Everything

One young lady thought she had nothing to live for because a successful mate would never come her way. She felt she'd be stuck with stragglers or losers. Out of despair she decided to be a prostitute and just have sex with anyone.

Women with low self-esteem are vulnerable candidates for prostitution. This woman's name was Yvonne. Not realizing that she had many skills other than sex, she chose prostitution as an effortless career where looks were not really necessary for success. In her words, "Who would hire someone like me? Only pretty girls get good jobs." She was wrong, but she was having her own pity party.

There are companies that hire people on the basis of looks, but the most prosperous and upstanding companies hire hard workers. They don't hire on the grounds of beauty, color, creed, or nationality. Good companies know it's training and initiative, not appearance, that determine success. Successful employees are what makes a company prosperous.

What happened to Yvonne has happened to many young ladies. She contracted the AIDS virus through unprotected sex. She gave it to several men, married and single. You can't see the AIDS virus with the naked eye, but you sure can feel it on your deathbed. It is a deadly and horrible disease that can cause its victims much suffering prior to death.

But Yvonne didn't get that far. Someone abducted her as she walked along the streets at night. He was a regular client with whom, in spite of all the special moves he would request, she felt comfortable. She was mistaken to feel that way. He drove her to a secluded location and shot her once in the head. She didn't have time to respond and try to save her life. It was all over just like that. Her body lay so long before it was found that when the coroner sat her up, she remained frozen in that position.

Dianna Cook Thomas

The coroner brushes the bugs and ants off of Yvonne's body.

Sure, life's hardships will get you down, but it's up to you to get up and do something about them. When you get up, be ready to tackle your problems. Remember, problems will always come your way. No one is exempt from dilemmas. Choose to go through them rather than go around them. Going through them makes you stronger for the next problem. When you go around them, you get a false sense of security because you can't see them anymore, but they are still back there, waiting to destroy you.

Proverbs 3:5, 6 says:

"Trust in the Lord with all your heart, and lean not on your own understanding; In all your ways acknowledge Him, and He shall direct your paths."

I'd rather be ugly, single, and disheartened than to suffer the consequences of Yvonne's choice. With protection and love, there is a quiet spirit that will help conquer all wrongs in your life. Ugly doesn't mean the end of your world. If you have to be ugly and unmarried the rest of your life, then so be it.

Sexual love is not the only kind of love in this world. There is also the love of friends and family, or the love of a child who needs a mentor, or the love of an elderly person who needs companionship. The list goes on and on. How about surrounding yourself with people who don't care about how you look?

Unconditional Love

Surround yourself with those who don't have to put you down just to make themselves look good. It's been said that blowing out someone else's candle won't make yours shine any brighter. Surround yourself with those who will accept you as you are, with or without material possessions. Most true friends were your friends when you had little. Think back!

No matter what young girls who wear little to no clothing may think they're saying I'm sexy, but instead they're sending a message that they are attainable, on display, and available for sex—but sex only. They are not communicating that they want an enduring, long-lasting relationship, or that they want to get to know someone casually before things get serious. When you get older, you can wear what you want, of course, but take my word for it. The message remains the same.

Girls, if you don't know a man and you go off with him, the battle is half lost. You will have put yourself in a position that will make it much harder for you to save yourself if he tries to harm or kill you. A man who won't wait does not deserve your friendship, let alone a relationship. Even those who will wait will sometimes give you a run for your money!

Now, there are a lot of honest and gracious men in this world. They don't harm you or anyone else. Most of the time they, too, will caution their cherished ones about the dangers in life, trying to safeguard their daughters, wives, mothers, and sisters. Ladies, they are not old-fashioned or trying to govern your life. They know that there is a small percent of humankind who are out for no good and some who are true monsters. Good men only want to spare you grief, injury, and pain and to save your life. Listen to them seriously and make a self-evaluation. Dress modestly or risk sending a dangerous message.

There are also a lot of caring, loving, and kind men who are faithful to their wives and family. A lot of men will help women if they see a crime occurring or see them in a crisis. The problem is that most criminals conduct their dirty work when no one else is around. They just wait for you to make a foolish mistake. That's what they count on. That's why it's very important to be safe, extra safe.

Respect Yourself

Yvonne felt that no one cared for her and that no one would want to be seen with her in public. She felt that men just wanted to use her. She said of herself, "I'm so withdrawn, so ugly, so homely. Why am I even here? I'm so depressed, and there is no bliss in my life."

She ate alone, slept alone, and the pain of hopelessness that she felt so deep within at times became unendurable. She was often the brunt of jokes and was looked down upon. It seemed to her that other girls had it made. She didn't know that inner beauty lasts so much longer and goes so much further than physical beauty.

Yvonne chose men to date who were losers. They beat her and put her down. She accepted this because she did not respect herself. Ladies, you don't have to live like this. There is nothing wrong with being alone. Your only choices are not to be a prostitute or to settle for less.

First Timothy 6:6 says, "Now godliness with contentment is great gain." Remember, contentment can be found in life's small pleasures, like flowers, green grass, trees, or the cute things that children do. Love and comfort come from the genuine gifts God sends like obliging and authentic friends. Bleakness comes to us all, even married couples, but soon passes if we face it head on. Don't ever think that your total happiness comes from someone else. There is nothing wrong with leading a single life and finding contentment in the love of family and friends.

People have to work at rediscovering happiness when feeling melancholy. It's best to turn to the simple things, like gardening, renting a movie to watch with a neighbor while eating popcorn, singing blissful songs, caring and sharing, traveling, or volunteering your services at a homeless mission.

Now, ladies, if you were to pass away today and were to look back on your life, you would regret all the time you exhausted worrying about a man, your clothes, how you looked, or the lack of money. Instead, you could have been beholding the world.

Here is some more food for thought. As you looked back, would you say to yourself, "I wish I'd spent more time at the office?" No, you would say, "I wish I'd spent more time doing the things that really mattered, like laughing more, and creating more happiness for others." You could have been manifesting life to the fullest. Have you been to Disney World, the Grand Canyon, Niagara Falls, the Alamo, or the Smithsonian? Have you been to England, China, Paris, Australia, Africa, or Hawaii? Have you eaten Cajun food in New Orleans? Have you gone to Shreveport in the springtime to observe the Azaleas? Now, that's living life to the fullest, as is kissing babies; or helping the elderly by sharing a meal with them or painting their houses; or going to the grocery store for someone experiencing hardship. Don't wallow in despair. Despair is the grave of dead hopes.

Don't give up. Do what's right, always. You can make it! That exhilaration will last a lifetime. If you fall into despondency, be cautious not to fall into a depression so bottomless that you'll have to seek psychiatric help. But if you do become hopelessly depressed, seek the help of a professional religious or medical counselor.

We are never the same each day. One morning I may awaken, go shower, brush my teeth, put on my uniform, and think, I'm being used on this job. I need to find another one. The next morning I may think, This is the best job that I've ever had. One day I may say, "I'm so glad I found my husband. I'm glad I'm married." Another day I may say, "Lord, if You e-v-v-v-v-er get me out of this marriage, You'll nev-v-v-ver have to worry about me marrying again." Some days children are fine—hugs, kisses, the sweet things that they say are so cute. Then, other days I may say, "I'll be glad when you're out of the house and grown."

Our minds are ever changing, and we should always remember that hardships are temporary, not a fixed conclusion. Yvonne fell into a depression so deep that she became a prostitute. It can happen to anyone.

Each one of us, whether we're presently cruising through the tranquil parts or struggling through the rough, has only one chance to live this life. If we literally accept the divine plan for us, we'll have the knowledge that frees us from depression and the low spirits of guilt and regret.

Isaiah 26:3 says, "You will keep him [or her] in perfect peace, whose mind is stayed on You, because he [she] trusts in You."

Chapter 4

I Can Live Again!

Because we are not angelic and because we all have our insipid moments, we often fall short of being the best that we can be, but as long as we're trying our best, we can be who we should be.

If your past is marked with wrong decisions and poor choices, learn from it. You can be your own best teacher. If your past is marred with sin, it can be self-detrimental and conscience hurting. But if you forgive yourself, it is the turning point toward a new and rejuvenated life. Make your past your pal and not your opponent.

Remember, no matter how bleak the night...believe in the coming of tomorrow. That is satisfactory enough! Psalm 30:5 says, "Weeping may endure for a night, but joy comes in the morning."

Satan Is a Defeated Foe

An art gallery displays in its window a painting of two people sitting at a desk, one a man with a distressed look of overwhelming pressure on his face. Sweat is pouring down his forehead, and he has a formidable look of defeat that encircles his presence. The other figure, Satan. Satan has the look of victory as he and the man sit over a finished game of chess. The man, it appears, has lost.

One day a businessman glanced at the painting while passing the art gallery. He stopped and began pondering the painting. He looked and pondered and looked and pondered. An experienced chess player himself, he finally screamed, "I've got it. There is one more move! There is one more move!" Ladies, it is never too late to live again, never. Even when your lows are at their lowest, there is always one more move.

That's what happened to Meagan. Meagan was married and had two children. Things went well in the first few years of marriage. Meagan and her husband, Jonathan, had it all—a nice home, two nice cars, and they went places together as a family should.

Meagan would ask Jonathan, "Will you love me when I'm old and ugly?"

Jonathan's reply, "Well of course I do...!"

They often laughed and played with one another, but things started to change. Jonathan started to become abusive toward Meagan. At first the children hardly noticed. Then, as time went on, Meagan and Jonathan argued and fought not only at home but in public as well. She and her children were forced to go to the YMCA shelter for abused women on two different occasions. The stay seemed unnatural at first. Then, after staying there for a short period of time, she decided that she had to make a living for herself and her children.

The thought of self-sufficiency was something she dreaded because her spouse had been her caretaker for years. She felt hindered by poverty, obscurity, and loss of prestige. Meagan even felt at times that divorce was an unpardonable sin and that she would be rated as a second-class citizen. Divorce is pardonable, and many people have been happier being divorced and single or in a second marriage than they have been in their entire life. Remember, God hates divorce, not divorced people.

So Meagan fought the battle. She caught two buses each way to work. When she finally got a place of her own and everything seemed to be sailing along, her utilities were cut off. She and the children had to do their cooking, cleaning, and homework in the daylight hours because there weren't any lights in the house at night. Meagan gained fifty pounds. Makeup couldn't cover the stress lines in her face, so she stopped wearing it at all.

To add to the stress, it seemed that if one child wasn't sick, the other one was. She became so depressed and fatigued that she would chew her nails to the quick, and her attitude was that of an unfriendly bulldog. What would she do? What could she do? She felt demoralized. She never seemed to catch up. She was at her lowest. If it wasn't for the trust in her children's eyes, she would have felt that she just couldn't keep going. She had nothing, but that was better than the beatings and the late-night weeping she had once endured.

Sex For Money Is Not a Solution

Then she had one more move. Another alternative. Either she could choose prostitution and making ends meet, or faith with more days longing, struggling, and being without. The fact of the matter is, she shouldn't have to choose. But Satan wants us to think that we do. Will your distress drive you to despair and disillusionment? Where will you find your strength? Psalm 121:1-2 says, "I will lift up my eyes to the hills—from whence comes my help? My help comes from the Lord..."

Meagan's final move was toward faith and determination to overcome. She still had her dignity to lose, and that was worth the struggle. She had two children who beheld her with innocence and admiration. The choice she made was the same one she would want her children to make someday when they were older and the going got tough.

Soon Meagan's final move led to better choices. These better choices led to better opportunities, and better opportunities led to better conditions. Now, she gets her hair and nails done again. She takes long walks to control her weight, and she is a much more benevolent person to those she comes in contact with, whether rich or poor. Her children are taken care of and even help out around the house.

Dianna Cook Thomas

The flowers seem prettier and the grass greener. Finally, she has serenity of mind, heart, soul, and body, not to mention a stable career. Her final move led to more hard times, and it would have been easier, at the time, to choose to sell herself for much needed cash, but the long-term payoff of prostitution is only more prostitution, and a "dead end" career.

My friend Tracy and my grandmother, Grandma Doshie, are about the strongest women I know. My best friend raised three children alone, and my grandma raised nine children alone. My grandfather left her to raise nine children all by herself. She had five boys, my dad being the oldest, and four girls, in that order. She worked two jobs that paid no more than $1.75 an hour. Never did prostitution enter into her mind as a choice of providing for her family. She is now highly respected by her children, and they will travel miles and miles just to be at her side.

Grandma has remained single—and happy—for years. As a matter of fact, she wouldn't have it any other way. I've tried to encourage her to date a couple of times, and she told me where I could go. If she could raise nine children by herself, then I know others can do it as well, for the more we struggle, the stronger we become, especially when God is involved, which He was in my grandma's life.

The book of Proverbs has much to say about the pursuit of wisdom. "But whoever listens to me [godly wisdom] will dwell safely, and will be secure, without fear of evil" (Proverbs 1:33). The entire Psalm, Psalm 91, promises protection for you, as a single mom, and your children, and for anyone else. (I encourage you to read it daily.)

I have worked prostitution detail as an undercover police officer in the past. At first I didn't want to do it—afraid my church members might think I had an extra job on the side. However, the agents assured me that they wouldn't let anything happen to me if at all possible. So I worked in the worst part of town with three other female police officers.

Not until I worked this detail did I understand how much prostitution is glamorized on television. Mentally and physically, I felt dirty, even just faking the career. The area was not clean, it was dark and scary.

I Can't See the Azaleas
True Crimes Against Women and Children

A smell of filth was in the air and trash was on the street. I assure you, I would rather live in dark houses without electricity, gas, and food, than to go through that turmoil. My clientele ranged from men in ragged pickup trucks to men in suits driving a Lexus. Some had wedding bands on and some didn't. One even had his small child in the car.

To make this operation worse, I had to sell my soul for a total price of $5.00 for oral sex. That's right: $5.00. Not thousands of dollars like the television shows claim. After you're commanded to perform all kinds of somersaults and splits in bed, you'd probably make a total of $10.00 or $15.00 per night. Frankly, my dear, I'd rather dig ditches.

Remember, struggles are only temporary. Always strive for success the clean and honest way. Ladies, one of the most tragic temptations in all the world is discouragement. Unless it is overtaken, it can become the cause of many ailments. It may even invite defeat by stifling ambition which, in turn, opens the door to envy and resentment that will eventually lead to dissipation. Being too downhearted to stand up for what is right may lead you to fall for anything.

Jesus said, "In the world you will have tribulation; but be of good cheer, I have overcome the world" (John 16:33).

While you are being buffeted by contrary winds, think to yourself how smooth the sailing is the majority of the time. Don't waste time over what you can't change. Look ahead and have hope. Keep going. When you face a temptation, may your faith give you the durability to grip the oars a little tighter!

> To look around is to be distressed,
> To look within is to be depressed,
> To look up is to be blessed.

Life has its obstacles. It's piled high with tribulations, but women have to overcome them. The biggest obstacles are little faith and big fear. Leaving an abusive relationship is tough because, as you have seen, the struggles can be troublesome, but don't let that stop you if you choose to leave. There are also struggles and afflictions in a sound marriage, but they can be withstood when both partners can communicate effectively or will seek professional counseling.

Abuse is not to be withstood. The struggles you face by leaving an abusive relationship are short term. Death or serious injury at the hands of an abusive partner is permanent.

Once you are out on your own, choose an honest career to support you and your children. Please don't choose dead end careers. I'm not talking about how much money a job pays. I'm talking about how the job makes you feel about yourself. Remember, as Francis Bacon stated, "The lame man who keeps the right road outstrips the runner who takes a wrong one."

It's About Your Legacy

Keep in mind that you are not living for your pleasure. You are living for your children. What you instill into them reflects on you later. You see, our children are copies of us. If we want our children to be honest, we must be honest. If we want them to be truthful, we must never tell them a lie. If we want them to be sensitive to the needs of others, they must see us help the poor and the sick, the destitute and the downtrodden. If we want to guard them from becoming alcoholics, they must see us drink responsibly—or not at all. If we want them to be self-supporting, we must teach them to work. If we want them to be law abiding, we must abide by the law and demand obedience from them. And if we want them to go to church, we must attend with them.

Children learn from their parents. If you want monsters, just ignore them. Send them to their room and shut the door. Do your own thing and let them do theirs. Curse and slap them around if you're in a bad mood and they cross you. Lie to them. Let them roam the streets and be with whomever they desire. Just remember, it will come back on you. A child who isn't wanted at home may be wanted in several states!

When I was about six years old, my grandfather had a vegetable garden that consisted of an assortment of things. The neighbor's chickens would often crawl under the fence and into his garden. It was so much fun trying to chase them out as we ran around the yard. We never got to touch them because, when they became trapped, they would jump over the fence as their wings flapped and feathers flew.

I Can't See the Azaleas
True Crimes Against Women and Children

My grandfather would always make the statement, "One day I'm going to kill those chickens." One day I thought to myself, Well, why don't I win his favor and do it myself?

After that, I waited and waited for the next chicken to crawl under the fence. Finally, the morning came. It must have been cool outside, because I remember wearing my jacket as I chased the chicken around the yard all by myself. Finally, I had him cornered. I took off my shoes and hit him in the head a couple of times. The chicken lay still, and I thought that it must be dead. I'd leaned forward just to make sure when all of a sudden the bird and its feathers shook violently for the last time. It scared the daylights out of me.

Oh, what a joy I felt as I ran and told my granddaddy that I'd saved him the effort of killing that chicken. I felt a little weary as I ran to tell him. It was just something I couldn't explain. I'd just saved him the time and effort in the hope that he'd love me more. But I also couldn't help feeling that I'd done something terribly wrong.

I explained to my grandfather what I'd done with a mixture of pride and guilt. My grandfather stared at me with an awestruck expression as he realized that I had taken his casual remark literally.

What he told me next has stayed with me to this day. In a kind voice he said, "Dianna, I didn't mean it that way. I was only talking. We must ask God for forgiveness because we've done wrong. Hurting any of God's creation is wrong, and we want to do what is pleasing to Him." Proverbs 18:21 says, "Death and life are in the power of the tongue..."

Wow! I felt like I had just committed murder, but I learned two important lessons. First, listen to your intuition. I'd had a feeling that what I was doing was wrong. Second, my grandfather used the incident to teach me that we must admit our mistakes and ask for forgiveness.

What we, as parents, do and say in front of our children does not disappear in thin air. Children absorb it like a sponge, especially when they are just observing us and we think they are not listening. We must correct them when they are small. Have little conversations with them. Admit and correct your own faults and explain to your children what you are doing.

Dianna Cook Thomas

You can face up to this responsibility when your children are young, or you can deal with the consequences when they're older, and you're bailing them out of jail. That is, if the bail isn't too high. Always remember that!

Chapter 5

I'm Too Smart

    A person who has been given a keen, brilliant mind has the potential for exemplary achievement. But this alone is not the whole story. More must be said, for you can have a head full of brains and still be woefully deficient in judgment and practicality. A woman can have all the education in the universe, but unless she has common sense with a predisposition for avoiding danger, she'll lose the battle.
    Supposedly educated college girls are so often caught off guard that I just want to shake them and say, "Wake up, this is the real world." I understand that they are learning how to live without the constant supervision of their parents and that dorm life gives them a sense of freedom, but psychopaths prey on their nonchalant attitudes and their bubbliness. Even though they are surrounded by peers who are interested in the same goal, an education, women students should not be lulled into thinking that they are safe on campus. Danger is everywhere, and the more we realize that fact, the more we can become defensive with every step we take.

Dianna Cook Thomas

Sometimes I get the feeling that there is a particular type of madman who, because he never has a good parent or never could learn to appreciate the devotion and security of an honest and well-balanced home, wants to take the exhilaration away from a girl who appears to have everything going for her. Whatever motive these monsters may have, women students need to be as cautious as possible. Unfortunately, female college students who become victims of violent crime often end up dropping out of school. They become unable to carry on their studies at the same time they are trying to cope with the anxiety and embarrassment caused by the attack.

Mind, Body, and Spirit

Intelligent women take care of their bodies as well as their minds. A middle-aged female, resourceful, athletic, and full of life, was jogging one morning. She was content as she started out on her jog down a known trail. Her mind was clear and refreshed. With each stride, she was preparing for the challenges of the day ahead. Then, out of nowhere, a car drove up. The passenger grabbed her and forced her into a car as it drove off. It happened instantaneously because it was planned.

Did you know that on some streets or paths it takes little effort for a passenger to snatch you with one hand, use his other hand to cover your mouth, then push you into the vehicle? That's what happened in this case. The passenger grabbed her, and the driver was ready to immediately drive away. It took every bit of ten seconds.

This poor girl was raped by both men and left in the timberlands bare and miles away from her jogging path. She had no cell phone, and there were no nearby neighbors. She was left feeling bewildered, belittled, and dirty. Even though she was horrified, she was relieved they didn't kill her.

Do you have a plan? Do you jog near a wooded stretch, or is there an isolated section on your path where you could be grabbed? Think about your route, and plan evasive actions you can take if someone approaches you.

Shantel's Story

No one knows if thinking ahead could have helped Shantel. Shantel was at a nightclub with her sister, Lanna. Both were smart and energetic. Shantel decided to go outside to smoke with a seemingly nice fellow. When she failed to return after a few minutes, Lanna began to look for her. Everyone wondered, What could have happened to Shantel? Did she go off on a one-night stand or has she been kidnaped?

Minutes turned into hours, and her parents and the police looked all night. They all knew that she was grown and had a life of her own, but at least she could have called family members to let them know where she was. Hours turned into days, and days into weeks.

Weeks later, children playing in a field near a wooded area a few miles from Shreveport noticed an old house and decided to see what was inside. There they found a badly decomposed body and notified their parents. The parents called police, and the police tried to decipher the cause of death. The authorities had an even bigger problem. The body was unidentifiable, which meant that a forensic pathologist would have to identify this Jane Doe through dental records.

It was Shantel. She was remembered as being gorgeous, ingenious, and endearing. The family was so hurt, having to wonder not only why she died but how she died. They blamed themselves and one another. I can't begin to tell you the psychological consequences that the family has suffered. Oh, if only Shantel had it all to do over again, what would she do differently?

Ladies, protect yourselves now. Remember the song, "If I could da, would da, should da?"

"Oh, if I could turn back the hands of time, I would have done things differently." We have all said it. "I should da been more mindful." Do it now and live. Strangers can't harm you if you outsmart them. They just move on to someone who presents an easier target. Never have so many drinks that you can't function in a normal fashion. Crime happens when you least expect it.

Dianna Cook Thomas

Louise

What about a place that seems the least likely in which a violent crime could occur, a shopping mall? It happened to Louise. She window-shopped alone that day, but in a well-known store. A gentleman spoke to her. She didn't speak back. She shopped a little while longer and then proceeded to another store. She didn't know that the same gentleman was anticipating an opportunity to catch her alone. He knew that even on his best day she wouldn't take a second look at him. He knew that the only way he could have her would be to force her. That is exactly what he and his acquaintances did.

These predators aren't interested in a relationship, girls. They want instant satisfaction. She went into a restroom without a clue of what was about to happen. Two other men who were used as lookouts assisted with the abduction. One grabbed her and took her into the men's restroom to the rear stall. All three men took turns raping her. They dared her to scream. But this was supposed to be an innocent shopping day. It was for the rapists! They didn't care if their victim was traumatized for the rest of her life.

Ladies, they don't care. Again, ladies, they don't care. Again, ladies, they don't care. You have to care about yourself. Only you can preserve yourself. Only you can care enough to live as safely as possible. You owe it to yourself and to those who love and need you.

Don't ever exclusively depend on mall security, or any security personnel for that matter, for your welfare. Make sure there are several people around as you enter into a restroom. Never assume a subject is alone or that you can never be harmed in a public place just because you're alone.

I must admit, when I started my research for this book, some of the horror stories that I read about women and girls startled even me—a ten-year veteran police officer. On one occasion, I was at a college library in a small, muffled room reading about a man who had broken into a lady's house and severely beat and raped her before stabbing her numerous times. Then, he kicked her in the face, disfiguring her for life. After that, he left her for dead. While I was taking notes, someone came to the all-glass door, and I suddenly looked up and screamed. I thought it was the suspect coming after me.

Then, I felt ridiculous, because it was the library janitor, whom I've known for several years.

I'm not insinuating that you must walk around in life being apprehensive. But all fear isn't bad fear. It can be good to have enough fear to want to live. Policewomen will be the first to tell you that no one is exempt from harm or death, not even us. In Baton Rouge, a policewoman and a manager of a grocery store were making a deposit when both were gunned down in an ambush. The manager lived. The policewoman, who had several small children, died. In addition to being a veteran police officer and a smart woman, she was a single mom and a dedicated worker.

It didn't matter to the suspects that she was in a police uniform, and it didn't matter that her children would grow up motherless. It didn't matter that she put her life on the line so that the citizens of Baton Rouge would be safe from the maniacs that she arrested. After it is all said and done, an apology from the suspect can't nurture her children. You apologize when you step on someone's toe or accidentally bump into them. You don't apologize when you kill someone.

Vanessa Learned the Hard Way

When we say that someone is a "smart" woman, we can mean two different things. We can mean "smart" as in "intelligent," like the women I've been telling you about. Or, we can mean "smart" as in "attitude." Both can get you into trouble. Vanessa was a young girl with a smart attitude. She was only sixteen years old when she decided that her life would be better without her mother telling her what to do.

Vanessa dreamed of falling in love with someone and of someone falling in love with her. I can remember being in love at a young age. My mom couldn't tell me anything. You see, love is stimulating. And blinding. "I love you, you love me," most of us have been there, or will be someday.

Vanessa was tired of her mom repeating, "If you're not obedient, Vanessa, you're gonna have a hard life." Mom would also say, "Vanessa, stay away from that boy, he don't mean you any good." But Vanessa wouldn't listen. Mom, Vanessa felt, was prehistoric (fortyish) and old-fashioned. Mom would often try to select her friends for her. She never chose the one who craved recreational activities with the boys, if you know what I mean. No, Mom always appointed the girl who just didn't have a clue to be her friend. Vanessa also had a problem with dress codes. "I want to wear my short shorts," whined Vanessa. This was something she and her mother argued over repeatedly.

Finally, Vanessa became so insistent that Mom at times would compromise just to have some tranquility. She had endured so many countless days and nights of Vanessa's prowling out with older men, smoking pot, sassing, coming home late, rolling her eyes at any convenient moment, talking on the phone until the early hours of the morning, being late for school, bringing home bad grades, and so on.

The more Vanessa's mom compromised, the more Vanessa would do things that challenged Mom's conservative and traditional way of life. Vanessa's mom finally decided that since Vanessa was so far out of hand, she would have to learn the error of her ways the hard way. Mom had been feeling only fear and grief as she watched her daughter denounce her faith and rush into sin. She had only hope to cling to.

Vanessa couldn't appreciate her affectionate mom. She wanted what she wanted and when she wanted it, and it had to be her way. Vanessa would periodically say, "When I have children, I'm not going to be like you, Mom. You'll see." Well, while still in high school, Vanessa became pregnant. Mom was grieved and disheartened. Of course, the baby's father didn't stay around long enough to know that she was pregnant, let alone to see what the baby's name would be. Vanessa named the newborn baby girl Abigail. Vanessa thought that getting pregnant and having a baby would demonstrate how much she loved her boyfriend and that he, in turn, would really love her.

Vanessa was abandoned with a baby to take care of for the next eighteen years, and oh yes, those girls who didn't have a clue, they went on to a higher education after high school. They were that different kind of "smart." But Vanessa wasn't humbled after having Abigail. She was still her kind of "smart." She became even more naughty. Vanessa thought that since she had Abigail, Mom really couldn't instruct in anything. Vanessa felt that she was just as grown as her mom. Ceaseless disagreements took place.

Then Mom finally had enough. "Get out, Vanessa, and find your own place by the first of the month."

"My pleasure," answered Vanessa smartly.

Shortly after moving out, Vanessa met Bill. Bill was your average twenty-one-year-old kid without a dime in his pocket, but he knew all the right words.

"But I love him, and he loves me and Abigail," Vanessa sighed. Bill didn't work. But he loved to baby-sit—and play music all day and night. Ultimately, it led to Vanessa's being evicted from her apartment, and Vanessa was pregnant by Bill.

One night in March 2000 while Vanessa and her friend Nicole looked for a place to live, Bill stayed home with two-year-old Abigail and two other children, a twenty-three-month-old and a three-year-old. Bill decided to take all three children swimming, so he got them dressed and started down the stairs. He picked up the twenty-three-month-old and allowed Abigail to follow behind down sixteen stairs. At about the twelfth stair, Abigail lost her footing in her Grinch house shoes and fell all the way down the rest of the stairs. Bill asked her if she was all right, and she stated, "Yes." She then stated, "I want to go potty."

Bill took them back up the stairs so she could potty, and she began to vomit. Bill again asked her if she was okay. And she again stated, "Yes." Abigail began to slowly lose consciousness. Bill picked her up and shook her, saying, "Wake up! Wake up!" Then he put her in the shower to wake her. She kept going in and out of consciousness. Then Bill called 911.

Paramedics arrived to find Bill shaking Abigail and yelling, "Are you all right? Come on, Abigail, don't go to sleep." The paramedics immediately insisted that Bill stop shaking her. They placed the child down and began to take her vital signs and give her much needed treatment. Bill repeatedly told a confused story to the paramedics as Abigail was transported to the nearby hospital Emergency Room. There she was expedited into emergency surgery.

Vanessa was contacted, and she hastened to be at her baby's side, imagining that Abigail probably had a bump on her head. As she sat anxiously in the waiting room, Bill doggedly tried to explain to Vanessa what had happened to Abigail. But there was no articulation of sorrow or mortification, just a continuous nagging conversation.

Detectives were notified by the hospital staff, as was Child Protection. Detective Patricia responded to the call.

This must be standard, especially when a child appears to be wounded, Vanessa thought. As the doctor entered the waiting room, Vanessa began to explain to him how habitually clumsy Abigail was. She was always falling.

"Vanessa, your daughter is dead," explained the doctor."

"What?" she screamed and screamed. Vanessa's family members and friends tried to console her as the doctor sauntered out, never offering an expression of condolence to Vanessa.

When the doctor talked to the detectives, he revealed to them that Abigail had had monumental brain mutilation, retinal hemorrhaging, a brownish contusion on the forehead, a circular discoloration around the umbilical area, deep stellate anal fissuring observed, anal fresh bleeding, bruises on the back, and a three-pattern circular bruise on her arm that resembled cigarette burns. The detectives told Vanessa, and she was grossly petrified. Totally. Further, a forensic investigation revealed that Abigail's #11 rib was broken and she had a lacerated liver.

After all was said and done, Bill was arrested for first degree homicide. Vanessa soon realized that Mom had been right all along. Vanessa had been safeguarded as a child, but she hadn't extended this care to herself or her child.

Mom always said, If I wasn't obedient, my life would be hard, Vanessa thought. But I'm too smart to have let this happen.

Now she was left with a dead child and pregnant by the man who was responsible for her daughter's death.

I Can't See the Azaleas
True Crimes Against Women and Children

No parent should ever have to go through this. Abuse is not only serious, but deadly.

Chapter 6

I'm Smart Enough To Discipline and Train My Children

A study estimated 50,000 cases of Shaken Baby Syndrome occur each year. Shaken Baby Syndrome results from shaking an infant or a small child by the arms, legs, chest, or shoulders. Even though Abigail's case was not consistent with Shaken Baby Syndrome, Bill had done some substantial damage to Abigail's brain by shaking her so brutally. A baby's head and neck are extraordinarily vulnerable to injury because the neck muscles haven't fully developed.

Children who are shaken do not necessarily sustain distinguishable, physical impairment, but when injury does occur, it can be irreversible or even fatal. The degree of brain damage a child may receive depends on the amount and duration of the shaking, as well as the force sustained by the head on impact. When the brain cells are damaged, there is no way to regenerate new ones. Therefore, the effects of most of these types of injuries are irreversible. The most common triggering event for shaking is constant crying. If your frustration level reaches the breaking point due to a child's crying:

- Abstain and place the child in a safe place.
- Calm down. If you can't settle down by yourself, call a friend.
- Try again to help the child.

If you suspect someone is hurting a child in this manner, call and get help immediately, even if you're not sure. Symptoms that indicate a child may be the victim of Shaken Baby Syndrome are:

- Partial or full paralysis
- Behavior problems
- Blindness
- Brain damage
- Seizure disorders
- Swallowing disorders
- Developmental disabilities
- Hearing impairments
- Autism
- Cognitive impairments

Parents, we should never stop raising our teenage children. They are not our friends. They are our responsibility, and they must be taught morals and ethics repeatedly and early in life.

Many times when responding to a call at any given house, I can tell who's been raising their children and guiding them in the right direction and who hasn't as soon as I walk in the door. Just the fact that a parent has to call the police for an obedience problem says a lot.

We can tell if a child has been properly disciplined from the age of two to seventeen, or if parents have waited until the child was a teenager to try to reprimand him or her. You can't do the latter, for then it's too late. Proverbs 22:6 says, "Train up a child in the way he should go, and when he is old he will not depart from it."

As officers, we witness challenges with rebellious children almost on a daily basis. Whether one works or has chosen to be a homemaker doesn't matter. Discipline is discipline. Children as young as toddlers need to learn obedience. If you don't teach them, just where in the world do you think they will learn it? The police? The schoolteacher? In reality, most police officers and teachers don't have any interest in or patience with a disobedient child.

If a child does not obey you as a parent, they will obey neither a police officer, teacher, preacher, neighbor, jailer, bondsman, judge, nor their bosses. Nor will they obey rules or regulations. The end result will be death or jail. Parents must sacrifice the time and cultivate the patience that it takes to properly discipline their own children, whether they live with them or not.

I'm from the old school and believe in spankings. I don't believe in "Time Out" or "Let's just talk to them." Spanking, however, must be supplemented with an explanation of what the child did wrong and what should have been done instead. Soon the spankings can cease, and you will only have to talk to them. True, every child is different, and every situation is different. You have to get children's attention and let them know who is in charge.

You shouldn't try to be friends with your children until you have established that concept. I don't believe in severe beatings because no child should conform to that type of punishment. It only creates monsters. There is a difference between chastisement and child abuse. Chasten children while they are young, and you'll have far fewer problems when they are older. Would you rather take the time to do the discipline, or would you rather a judge and jury do it for you?

Remember, parents, it doesn't matter how tired we get of the responsibility of our children. They are ours forever. Children must be made to understand that parents know what's out there on the streets and are trying with all their heart to educate them about the mean and cruel world.

Wise Women

Parents have more experience and intelligence than young daughters and sons presume. But there is that time in a sixteen-year-old's life when Mom is considered an intruder and behind the times. Mothers want to save their children the grief and torment that life oftentimes will bring. She can only tell you what's right and wrong. You will have to encounter many things yourself, especially if you're rebellious and certain that you can make better choices than your elders.

In other words, life can be complex enough on a good day, so don't make it more complicated. The more parental instruction a daughter has, and a good and firm foundation to stand on, the better equipped she will be when the road gets rough. Believe me, girls, it invariably does. Absolutely no one can escape life without trials and tribulations. It's like my police job. The more training an officer has, the better the chances he or she has of surviving. That's a fact.

Mom can give you the training, but it's up to you to make good use of that training when life brings hard times. A bad experience can be so overwhelming that it becomes lethal one way or the other.

Remember Mom or Dad, set standards in your home by drawing the line. Children, whether adolescent or adult, must respect parents. Inappropriate behavior should not be tolerated. Don't let them push the limits. If you don't approve of smoking, foul language, or boyfriends or girlfriends, they should not be allowed inside your home.

My friend, Linda, who works in the Neo-Natal Intensive Care Unit at a local hospital, says the mothers are becoming younger and younger. She remembers a twelve-year-old having a baby. One thing is certain. That mom doesn't have to worry about finding a pediatrician. She already has one—her own.

Rebellion

A pregnant teen can be one problem in the home, but what about a young child who is so rebellious that he drives you up the wall? The next story describes just such a child. This rebellious young child just couldn't take the chastisement of his mother, so he ran away from home with friends who felt the same as he did.

Night drew near, and they knew it was time for sleep. After all, this preplanned event took brains. The four friends decided to sleep between train tracks to keep warm. Suddenly a huge train whistle signaled for the boys to run. They did. All but one made it. What happened? He was run over by the train, splitting him in half. Smart enough to be on your own? These boys were not smart enough to be on their own.

One day my son, Jabari, was upset because things weren't going his way. At the age of five, he felt money grew on trees. With tears in his eyes and his bottom lip poked out, he stated poignantly, "I'm running away, and you'll never find me."

"Why?" I asked curiously.

"Because you won't give me that drum set I want."

"Just how are you going to get there?" I queried.

"The Ground Hog!" he exclaimed defiantly.

"Don't you mean the Greyhound?" I countered.

What should you do if your child threatens to leave home? Talk to them and let them know that the dark streets aren't friendly like they seem. They'll have no shelter over their heads, no money for food, and most of all, no one to protect them from those who are much stronger than they are. When your child goes to bed at night, check on them often because peer pressure can be strong.

The next story tells of an unruly teenager who finally broke the camel's back and received punishment that was much too harsh. When Marie and Richard got married, Marie had a small child from her previous marriage. Richard raised Marie's son, Courtney, from the age of three. Marie had some apprehensions about Richard spanking Courtney and often intervened.

Courtney got more and more out of hand as the rebellious years progressed. At age fifteen, Courtney and some friends decided to break into a car and steal the stereo equipment. Marie and Richard received a knock on the door from the police with a warrant for Courtney's arrest. Richard was embarrassed beyond description as the neighbors looked on.

After Richard bailed Courtney out of jail and got him home, he was still enraged and whipped Courtney with an extension cord. Marie, equally displeased with Courtney, held her tongue this time. What else were they to do with him? If he got away with car burglary, murder may be next. Was Richard too angry to chastise Courtney? Was talking to Courtney going to do any good when it had failed in the past?

Many government agencies do not want citizens to spank their children at all. However, when they become teenage monsters, there aren't enough Boot Camps to go around, and the monsters are the parents' problem. As the pictures reveal, Richard had gone overboard and subsequently he was arrested for abuse.

Teenage children will make a priest weep. Nowadays, there is no such thing as spanking, and by the time children become juveniles, they may be whipping their parents. I've had to make several calls where parents have called the police for an uncontrollable child. Never punish a child when your emotions are out of control. No child deserves that. Years of bitterness well up within the parent, and punishment turns into abuse. Courtney is a victim now, but when he gets older, he will victimize another, whether a child, a wife, or an innocent citizen, and thus the cycle repeats itself.

Teens, let me give you some solid advice. Understand that parents are not perfect human beings. There are no perfect human beings. Hence, learning to adhere to rules and obey laws are essential to leading a productive life and maintaining a functioning society. That's why parents are trying to train you while you are young. While in training, you are being molded to understand how to live a successful life. Otherwise, you will stigmatize yourselves as rebellious oddballs. There is no glory in being different for difference's sake.

Parents may seem wrong though triumphant in most situations, but there is always a reason for everything, and the end result when obedient is always success.

Home Should Be Where the Heart Is

Your home shouldn't be a filling station, a debating society, or a boxer's ring. A home is a place to be loved and the first place to learn life's lessons. Like the little birds that grow up and leave the nest, children grow up and depart taking everything they have learned from home with them, whether good or bad.

If you've learned patience and love, you'll be patient and loving with your children and friends. If you've learned hate and disorder, your life will always have strife and disarray.

Chapter 7

I'm Smart Enough To Avoid Infant Abuse

Let's take Yanetta for instance. Yanetta was smart and had loving and kind parents who only wanted her to have a full and abundant life when she was old enough and out on her own. But no, Yanetta couldn't and wouldn't even try to understand their blueprint of morals and ethics, for she thought that she was smarter than her old-fashioned and outdated parents.

You see, to have a great life takes planned achievements that have to be carried out in a systematic way. While you're young, your parents decide your life, and when you become an adult, you decide your own life. Experience from home is your foundation. Rebellious Yanetta struggled through high school and then fell in love with a young man shortly after graduation.

College was what her parents wanted for her, and that alone was enough to put her off the idea. She became pregnant, and the test of life was about to begin. "What test?" you might ask. It was definitely not a college test. It was a test of how well she had internalized the morals and ethics taught to her as a child. Only time would tell.

Dianna Cook Thomas

    Her beautiful and precious baby girl was born in September 2001, and soon after the baby was born, her young prince found interest in other matters. Not all young men are like this, but a young father's good intentions can quickly dissolve, especially when a child is unplanned.

    Yanetta soon became exacerbated over the reality that she was saddled with this baby while the baby's father had taken his favors elsewhere. So she took it out on her cuddly, healthy newborn. About one-and-a-half months after her birth, the baby was admitted to the hospital. The doctor explained to Detective Patricia that the baby had been severely injured, and though still alive, would never be normal as long as she lived.

    What could have happened to a healthy newborn? Let's see, where shall we start? Try seizures, diarrhea, vomiting, and dehydration due to fractures to the legs and arms and specifically the left arm and radius and right femur. Injuries to the left femur, right tibia, a dislocated left hip and elbow. She had a shunt placed in her brain to relieve bilateral chronic subdural hemorrhaging (an old skull fracture that was causing the brain to bleed and subsequently caused the seizures).

    Yanetta, out of anger, had grabbed the baby every time she cried and shook her, which is an example of Shaken Impact Syndrome or the Shaken Baby Syndrome. The baby was repeatedly grabbed and shaken multiple times.

    Yanetta explained to Detective Patricia that she would pull and jerk on the baby while picking her up by the body, under her arms, and thus forcefully squeezing and shaking her to make her stop crying. She also stated that she used great force when hitting the baby in the back of her head with an open-handed strike. She admitted that she felt for the baby's soft spot on her head and squeezed it with her hand in a forceful manner.

    Yanetta stopped the abuse after about two weeks because the baby began to display jerking of the head and arms and her eyes began to roll back in her tiny head. She didn't do anything about the baby's suffering right away because she didn't want anyone to find out what she had done. Literally, days passed without getting the infant any medical attention. Detective Patricia felt so grieved inside for this little one, but she had to preserve a placid, professional demeanor.

    I include this particular story because many young girls aren't ready to become mothers, let alone single mothers. They only think they are ready. This advice I shall pass on to you. If you don't feel you're capable of handling the stress of motherhood, there is no shame in giving your baby to a foster home. You can also turn the baby over to the care of a police officer or a firefighter.

Of course, you know that not all single parents are mean and cruel. Even stepfathers can be the best thing that could ever happen in a child's life. Many children have been raised by their stepfathers, and these men have done an excellent job. Conversely, biological fathers can do some cruel things to their own flesh and blood, as you will see in the next story.

Who says grown men don't cry? What happened in the next scenario made the police and paramedics shed tears of bewilderment, grief, and bafflement. They went home at the end of the shift and hugged their own children tightly.

It all took place in the McKinney residence. Judy and Seth McKinney had dated for three years and had been married for two. They had a baby son adorned with precious innocence. Judy told Seth one night as she held her newborn in her arms, "I don't know what I would do without either you or my baby."

Dianna Cook Thomas

A mother of a newborn has to be one of the happiest individuals on the face of the earth especially when her baby is healthy. This little one awaits a life full of colorful Azaleas. Will he get to see them? Find out.

I Can't See the Azaleas
True Crimes Against Women and Children

Seth had continued to drink a little in spite of the newborn son, Donald. After all, no harm in that. Right? One night Judy did a few chores around the house while Seth drank. After Seth finished drinking, she decided to go to bed. Seth followed right behind her. Seth was very intoxicated, but Judy had no idea of what was about to happen. Seth got up to check the baby. The baby's monitor was turned up and Don hadn't cried. So why did Seth get up?

The next thing Judy knew, Seth was waking her up to tell her that something was wrong with the baby. Seth explained that he had gotten a paper towel and begun to wipe off the excess milk from Don's mouth. But Don would not stop crying. Seth said that he had just laid the baby back down in his crib and left the room. When he returned, he noticed that Don had stopped breathing. He tried to perform CPR on the baby while Judy called the paramedics. When the paramedics arrived, they worked on little two-month-old Don and transported him to a local hospital.

The police and detectives arrived to investigate this seemingly normal case after they received a phone call from the hospital. The examining physician revealed that someone had put a large piece of wadded-up paper towel in the baby's mouth and shoved it down his throat. Extensive head injuries indicated that the baby's caretaker must have thrown him.

It was discovered that Seth had become so engulfed with anger that he not only stuffed a wad of paper towels down the infant's throat, but he had also thrown him across the room into his baby bed. The baby hit his head on the rails of the bed and sustained severe skull damage. He also had suffered broken ribs in previous incidents. Some of the ribs had healed while others were in the process of healing.

This explained why Don cried continually. Seth had gotten angry previously and abused Don severely. Medical attention wasn't given because the mother was unaware of the abuse and thought the child was constipated. Seth, who knew the real story, wouldn't even seek help for his own two-month-old son. The child was bleeding from the anus as well, indicating possible sexual assault pending the findings of the autopsy.

Judy, even though she thought she did everything right, married the wrong man. As she looks back, the warning signs were there. Seth's ex-wife had loads of information about him that would have alerted Judy to be careful of her mate. A woman's worst nightmare came true for Judy. She lost her husband and child in one single night. She thought she'd only see her baby in his bed, never in a coffin.

When a newborn is in the house, marijuana and alcohol must be forbidden. Drugs and alcohol have taken away many innocent lives and have destroyed many families. It seems that citizens aren't getting the picture about the abuse of these substances, even when such innocent lives are taken away due to their consumption.

             I Can't See the Azaleas
      True Crimes Against Women and Children

The choice is up to you.

photos by Roger Courtney

Chapter 8

I'm Smart Enough Not To Drink and Drive

Alcohol and drugs should never be present when driving a car or caring for infants and children. Those two substances have ruined the lives of those who have used them as well as the innocent victims who have had to live with the substance abusers. I can't begin to tell you the number of fatalities I've seen that were caused by a drunk or chemically impaired driver. But people whose judgment is impaired by drugs or alcohol think they're smart. Just try to tell one of them that you're not going to let them drive.

No husband or father wants to lose his wife and children because of a drunk driver. Do you want to be the cause of destroying a family because of self-centered motives and self-indulgence? People seem to think that just because they can stand up and walk after having a few drinks they can drive. If they can stand up, they can walk. If they can walk, they can drive. They conclude that driving is the easiest part of their night of excitement. They never consider the peril awaiting them or some innocent victim.

Dianna Cook Thomas

Actually, hardly ever do you hear from those who have killed the innocent due to drunk driving. Most of the time you hear only from the victims' family members. Most people who have taken an innocent life through their negligence only wish they could turn back the hands of time. After the accident, that they themselves have caused, they only wish they had never placed a glass of alcohol to their lips. Especially when they've caused the death of a parent and three children ranging from two to six years old, an incident you'll hear more about later.

Just think, death because of carelessness, and the drunk driver walks away without a scratch, only a dreadful memory. Then, the once-drunk driver is forced to sit in jail and rot to death, oftentimes wishing he were lifeless instead of the innocent. Of course, there are those who couldn't care less if they've killed an entire family due to alcohol, as long as they get that smooth feeling. As a matter of fact, some are on their fourth DUI offense, and they have used being drunk and under the influence as an excuse for their troubles rather than the cause of them.

Men especially are hard to convince of the dangers of driving under the influence. After all, they are the better drivers! Have you ever heard the saying, "Those damn women drivers"? The two men I'll tell you about next thought like this.

Around twelve o'clock noon, in the broad light of day, two young gentlemen decided to go out for a ride. They'd been drinking for a while, but thought they could handle it. They had assured themselves, as a matter of fact, that they could handle it. After all, men are the better drivers, drunk or sober. Hence, a few beers and lots of laughs.

They figured they could get from point A to point B without running across the police, and no one else would notice who they were or what they were up to, let alone what their blood alcohol levels might be. After all, nothing had ever happened to them before while drinking and driving, so what could possibly befall them now?

They drove as cautiously and correctly as they could, signaling on all turns, stopping at all stop signs and red lights. It all seemed so fundamental. They would even take a sip or two of beer when no one was looking. If the driver seemed about to make a mistake, the passenger would help navigate him through, and that, within itself, made them feel confident as they laughed. The passenger knew that his life was at stake as well as the driver's. Even if they weren't thinking about the innocent lives they were endangering, they didn't want to lose their own lives.

    The driver made a foolish quick and sudden turn and an even more foolish attempt to get back to the other side of the road. On the following page, see for yourself. Then tell me, can you distinguish what kind of vehicle the drunk driver was in? You will get an A+ if you can!

    This scenario does not gear directly toward violence against women or children, however many have been victims of such acts. Many people have even placed their innocent children in their vehicles while drinking and driving and the end results were devastating. Stop drinking while driving before you run out of choices. If you drink, be responsible. When with a group, choose a designated driver. Having one person agree to drink only non-alcoholic beverages and provide transportation for other members of the group can save lives.

Here's a form of abuse in a different way. The abuse of alcohol, which can result in drinking and driving, can be fatal of one person or an entire family. Don't let your selfish abuse become someone else's tragic loss.

Here are some things you can do as a host to ensure responsible drinking at a social function:

- Stop the flow of liquor at least one hour before the party is over.
- Serve food to slow the rate of absorption of alcohol.
- Do not pressure guests to drink.
- Provide plenty of non-alcoholic beverages.

If a guest drinks too much, call a cab or arrange a ride with a sober driver. This may seem inconvenient, but it will be one of the best decisions you'll ever make as a host.

Remember, when you drive, you want to protect yourself and those you love. So, be alert and watch out for impaired drivers. Be aware of drivers who display these characteristics when on the road:

- Driving after dark with headlights off.
- Turning abruptly or illegally.
- Responding slowly to traffic signals.
- Braking erratically.
- Stopping without cause.
- Driving at a very slow speed.
- Driving on the wrong side of the road.
- Almost striking an object or vehicle.
- Weaving, swerving, drifting, or straddling the center line.
- Making wide turns.

We must continue to fight against drunk driving until the message is clear: If you drink, don't drive.

If you are serving alcohol at a party, think safety first. After all, drinking may be considered fun, but it isn't fun if you or someone you know gets hurt or killed as a result of it.

There is another type of car crash that appears to be increasing: crashes caused by drivers who are tired or fatigued. Hundreds of thousands of crashes annually are known to be caused by lack of driver attention, which is a symptom of sleep loss.

With today's busy lifestyles, people often get less sleep than they need. Sleepiness decreases driver awareness, slows reaction time, and impairs judgment. Don't think that you're too smart to succumb to the effects of fatigue. Here are some lifestyles and situations that put you at risk:

- A young driver. Young people tend to get less sleep than they need.
- A shift worker. Changing work schedules can make it difficult for your body to adapt.
- Taking medication that causes drowsiness.
- Driving on long, boring roads.
- A frequent traveler. Jet lag can cause sleepiness.
- Driving through the night or at other times when you would ordinarily be sleeping.
- Traveling long distances without taking breaks.
- Sleep deprivation.

The following tips can help you recognize the signs of fatigue, and they will help you to avoid becoming drowsy behind the wheel:

- Missing traffic signs.
- Having wandering or disconnected thoughts.
- Yawning repeatedly.
- Having trouble keeping your head up.
- Having to jerk your vehicle back into your lane repeatedly.
- Having difficulty focusing or keeping your eyes open.
- Tailgating the car in front of you.
- Not able to remember the last few miles.

If you experience any of these warning signs, use your common sense and good judgment to find a safe place to stop, rest, or sleep.

Never try to relieve fatigue (or depression) with alcohol, whether you're operating a vehicle or not. Haven't you heard that saying, "Driving will not solve a problem, it'll just make matters worse"? The next story is an extreme example of why.

Drinking to Solve Problems

Meridian, a young lady who seemed to have so many problems, turned to alcohol as an escape. One night, when already tired, she decided to have a few drinks.

As the night wore on and she had more drinks, she decided to take a nice long walk to try and sort things out. As she walked along the lonely and quiet streets in her neighborhood, she began to see where all her mistakes had started, but how could she undo what had already been done?

Meridian was weary and confused and needed to sit down as soon as she could. She found a spot on the railroad tracks. As she sat and pondered, she tried to think of a way to sort things out. She tried to put the pieces of the puzzle together in such a way that all the bad things would come together for the good.

Somehow, she couldn't hear a 100,000-ton freight train coming toward her. The sound starts so quietly when it's far away, and then it blends in with the rest of the sounds as it approaches. It's hardly noticed as it gets closer.

Suddenly, she looked up and there it was—an enormously huge train traveling like lightning. It was too late to react. Too late to change her mind. Alcohol was not the solution to her problems.

Most problems can be solved one way or another. If they can't be solved, change directions and move on. Alcohol is never an answer to your problems. When you're drunk, you not only have the original problem but also the problems that grow out of impaired judgment. When you're under the influence of alcohol, you are visually, audibly, and emotionally impaired. Problems should be dealt with one at a time, and most importantly, soberly.

Self-Indulgence Always Leads to Self Pity

Drinking never solves any of your problems. As a matter of fact, some of its outcomes can leave you worse than before. My next story is another tale of a violent act inflicted upon innocent victims. But it is not an abuse that is usually thought of as violence against women. I disagree. See what you think.

The story began with two people falling in love and deciding to spend the rest of their lives together. Kellie and Ray married in April of 1984. First son, Jeremy, was born on December 16, 1984. This first child was the apple of the happy couple's eyes.

Dianna Cook Thomas

Son Justin was born in October 1987. Both boys were little rascals. They loved to make noise, and the couple seemed to grow used to it. Then in June 1989 another son, Nicolas, was born. There was always something going on. Soccer, baseball, basketball, not to mention football, were the family's pastimes, and a way of saying, "We are caring and concerned parents."

They all attended church and Sunday school faithfully each week because Ray was the church musician.

One Saturday, Mom and Dad decided to visit in-laws because they knew that Monday would come only too soon and that meant back to work. Both had modest jobs, nothing to brag about, but they kept food on the table and paid the bills. They provided decent clothes to wear, and they were warm in the winter months and cool in the summertime.

So they packed up the family, and away they went. It was a family gathering. The weather was cool as it was fall. The leaves were turning brilliant red and dazzling yellow. The gathering was especially pleasant because they all got along so well together.

As 10:00 p.m. approached, it was time to head home and put the boys to bed. Jeremy was now nine, Justin seven, and Nicolas five. They had played long and hard with the other children, and they smelled like a room full of running backs. Everyone kissed and hugged goodbye. They loaded up the vehicle and waved as they left.

While Kellie and family headed west, Charles, age thirty-eight, was heading east. Charles had gone to work drunk earlier that day. His supervisor smelled the odor of alcohol as he stumbled into the facility. This was his last time to do such a thing because Charles had been warned that if he came to work drunk again he would be fired. Charles angrily left the facility only to go to the local bar and have more drinks and a pity party. Since he was divorced and had no one to go home to, he stayed in the bar drinking from 3:00 to 10:00 p.m.

Finally, he'd had enough and left before anyone could stop him. As he headed east, he crossed the double yellow line as he topped a hill. The family of five was quietly approaching the hill from the opposite direction. The impact was so explosive that Charles' vehicle landed on top of the family's vehicle.

Jeremy, the nine-year-old, suffered a dislocated shoulder but managed to get out and go for help. The paramedics and police arrived and airlifted Nicolas and

I Can't See the Azaleas
True Crimes Against Women and Children

Justin to a hospital. Ray, age thirty, died while being transported to the hospital. Kellie, also transported by ambulance, had two broken hips, a broken pelvis, and a broken left leg. She had to have four surgeries, one of which consisted of receiving eight plates to her facial area. By Sunday morning Justin, the seven-year-old, had died, and by Tuesday, Nicolas, age five, had died.

Kellie and nine-year-old Jeremy were the only survivors. Each faced months of recovery. Family and friends prayed. Employees of the companies where they had worked gave support, prayers, flowers, cards, and lots of love. That seemed to ease some of the pain.

While in severe pain and wheelchair bound with broken bones, her face in bandages, Kellie buried her husband and two young sons together. There was no life insurance and the car insurance company demanded to be repaid for hospital bills at once. This left the mother and son with only social security as a means of support.

Fortunately, there was a Psychiatrist who got Kellie through the ordeal. This Psychiatrist checked on her and her son's welfare day and night. It seems she felt comfortable lying on His couch and expressing her disappointments and frustrations to Him, and she was never overcharged or considered a burden in the late-night hours. Her son saw Him as well. Even though I don't like to name the name of a particular facility for fear of sounding biased, I strongly recommend Him. He has branches in every city, and I advise that if you ever have a problem, see Him. His name is Jesus.

Kellie explained to me during an interview that she never consulted with anyone but Him. Kellie even asked the insurance company to allow her to have that same family vehicle that was so horribly destroyed to be put in her backyard as a reminder. Bewildered, they granted her request. Today, she lives in the same house where she and Ray first lived after they were married.

Her house is so quiet now that she can hear the clock ticking on the wall. She only has memories of the everyday normal hubbub. It seems so unbelievable that the abuse of a drunk driver could almost wipe out an entire family. It was unplanned and sudden. There was no time to build that portfolio and to assure financial security.

Kellie is quite a lady. She feels that one day she will see them all again. She is determined to live

Dianna Cook Thomas

right and do that which is pleasing to the Lord. She attends the same family church. Jeremy is an honor student, and Kellie hasn't had a moment's trouble out of him.

    It would have been easier if she and Ray had financially planned for an uncertain future. Kellie and Jeremy had to do without many things, but God was faithful to His Word and made provision for their needs.

I Can't See the Azaleas
True Crimes Against Women and Children

This is an example of a beautiful home that is surrounded by the colorful Azalea.

photo by Roger Courtney

Chapter 9

I'm Too Rich

"If you have money, you can acquire anything."
"Wealthy people are snobs." Are you familiar with these assumptions? They are not always valid. A lot of wealthy people are not snobs at all. As a matter of fact, you'll never know they are rich until someone tells you. Then people look at them as though they were dollar signs instead of the congenial and authentic people you first knew them to be. Another untrue belief is that money can buy everything. It cannot.

The quiet canyons above Beverly Hills provide privacy and luxurious living just far enough from the glitter of Hollywood. In a home in one of these canyons, a rich woman was waiting to romance the man of her dreams, her husband Jonathan, who was in Europe on a business trip. But that day would never come for this rich cosmopolitan woman and her husband—the father of her only child.

This particular woman associated only with the prominent and sophisticated. She often held impromptu gatherings to keep from being bored and lonely. Though they had a locked gate approximately a hundred feet from the house, this couple's mansion was not completely secure. While home alone preparing for a gathering, something horrifying happened.

When guests arrived, something seemed wrong. No one answered when they knocked. How suspicious! they thought. They notified the police. When the police arrived, they found the woman lying on the floor with blood smeared all over her body and all over the walls. There was a rope around her neck. She was eight months pregnant.

Crime happens in every community on earth. Keep doors locked and secured and windows and blinds closed— no matter who you are and what you have. Remember, money can't restore your life once it is taken away. Money can't appease the pain of a child who has lost his mom. Nothing can replace the tender embrace and care of a mother.

Having money does not unravel crimes. In Boulder, Colorado, a young girl, under the protection of her parents, lost her life. The sumptuous lifestyle of her parents could not bring her back. Her life of innocence ended. While asleep, an attacker stole the life and all of its possibilities from a four-year-old angel. The opportunity to climb and jump, to chuckle and giggle, to be a cheerleader, to have a first embrace, to sneak and whisper on the phone to her sweetheart in the late hours of the night, to be a fashion model, and finally, to raise a four-year-old of her own one day, disappeared. Riches and fortune cannot cause a suspect to materialize.

A similar circumstance applies in the case of a wealthy victim and the rich alleged perpetrator from Greenwich, Connecticut. The body of a young girl from an affluent family was found not far from her parents' upscale chateau. The home was located in a neighborhood where doors are left unlocked. Privilege can lend people a false sense of security. The affluent get used to having things go their way. It's hard for them to believe their money can't protect them. Or failing that, bring a killer to justice.

But a killer lived for twenty-five years without being caught. Someone spent those twenty-five years with his or her affectionate family, going to their soccer games, ballet dances, and to the movies with friends, perhaps even attending church services on Sundays. No one has spent even a single day in jail for twenty-five years for the crime.

I Can't See the Azaleas
True Crimes Against Women and Children

Don't mistake wealth and social position for security. Danger is not specific to color, gender, having money or the lack thereof. Money isn't a ticket to absolute safety. Even the wealthy should always keep their doors locked. Protect your loved ones and yourself. A luxurious lifestyle is no good if you're dead. You can't see it or enjoy the material items that can be purchased with it. On the following page is a coffin of what I call $20,000 in the hole.

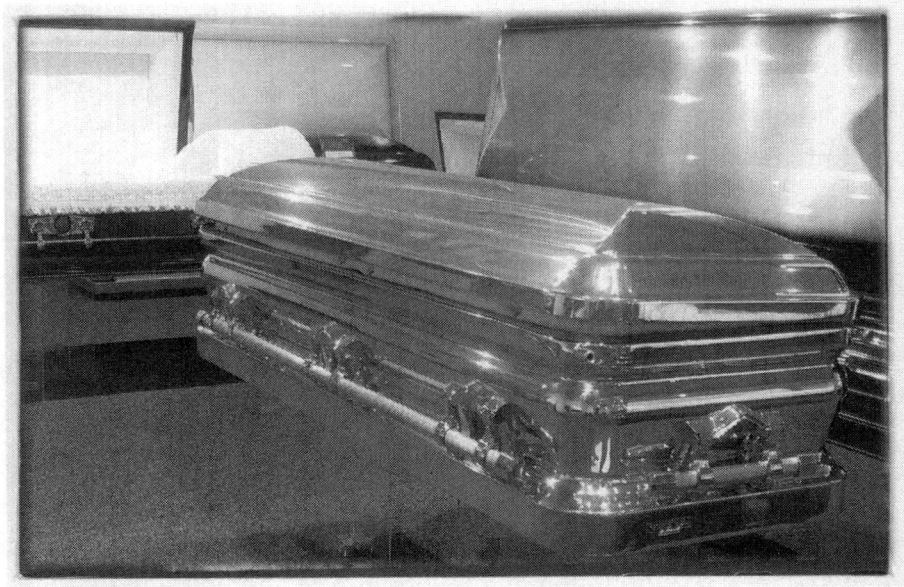

A $20,000 coffin and funeral expenses can be costly. Yet, it doesn't matter what you spend, the victim can't see the Azaleas. Please protect yourself.

Chapter 10

But I Trust Him

There are companions that women choose above their own children. Your mate loves you, but his love isn't always there for your children. Can he love you and not love your children? Is his love so unforgettable that it's worth the sacrifice of your children's innocence?

The next situation tells the story of little Buckey, then nine months old, who lived with his mom, Sharon, and her live-in boyfriend, David. In the beginning it was all passion and romance. David knew all the right things to say. But little Buckey acted distrustful of Mom's lover for some unknown reason. Mom disregarded little Buckey's reserve toward David, thinking he just needed to get used to her lover.

Little Buckey's stepfather, David, gave him hard liquor, straight, from the age of nine months. David and Sharon would laugh because it made little Buckey walk clumsily and act scatterbrained. They both thought it was entertaining. Even Sharon found it humorous because it made David smile.

David didn't have a job. He was a freeloader. Sharon was the one who worked. One day when she returned home from work, little Buckey whined that his arms were hurting. Sharon disregarded his whining since he was always complaining.

When Sharon's mother, Mrs. Vanessa, came over the next day, she became suspicious when she saw Buckey lying on the couch with an expressionless stare. He'd been asleep for several hours which anyone knows is peculiar for a small child. Mrs. Vanessa took Buckey to the hospital. She discovered that David had given Buckey some prescription medication containing codeine, something that could have severely injured or killed the child. It was later uncovered that Buckey had two broken arms and a broken ankle. The medicine had been given to camouflage the discomfort of the injuries, almost killing him.

Further tests showed that Buckey had a fractured skull, broken ribs, and bruises inside his stomach from being kicked. Child Protection Services didn't call the police at that time, but they did send the child to a foster home after he'd convalesced from his injuries.

A year passed and Buckey was doing fine. He had good and loving foster parents. He put some weight on his slight frame and began to chuckle and play as little children should. He was well cared for by his foster parents.

But the incomprehensible came to pass. Buckey was given back to his natural mom, Sharon. She had pleaded incessantly for his return, probably because she would receive compensation from the State if she were his guardian. There was a prerequisite, however. Sharon was ordered never to allow David to have access to Buckey.

Another Round

Within twenty-four hours, Sharon got an emergency phone call at work from the hospital. She hurried to the hospital to learn that Buckey had been injured. His baby-sitter was David. She not only took David back, but she left Buckey alone with him once again.

This time it was ascertained by the Emergency Room staff that Buckey had sustained second degree burns to the entire right side of his face as well as a burn to his tongue. The nail on his right ring finger had been completely removed, and he had been held down on an ant hill and had sustained bites over his entire body—the most serious under his armpits and in the groin area. He had suffered for hours with no medical care and was in a state of shock. Why did Sharon accept David back? Sharon was pregnant by David, and he told her that he wouldn't harm Buckey.

Detective Suzanne told Sharon that David's story did not coincide with the severity of Buckey's injuries. David had explained to Detective Suzanne that Buckey was a typical clumsy two-year-old child. Sharon told the Detective she believed David, not the doctor. Beforehand, David had explained to Sharon that Buckey was being his usual clumsy self.

Sharon's family had insisted over and over again to her that David was no good and that he did not care anything for her or little Buckey. He also beat Sharon from time to time, but that didn't seem to matter to Sharon. It was almost as if she accepted it as normal.

When the police interrogated Sharon, she had a nonchalant attitude regarding her son's mistreatment. She also displayed a total absence of a mother's natural instinct to protect her child. Her desire for David was more meaningful than the life of her child.

Sharon was arrested on her job, but David was harder to find. Every time the detective would go to his mom's house, David was gone. So Detective Suzanne played a psychological trick on him. She went to the projects where David was supposed to have been hanging out. In high crime areas, African-Americans sometimes won't give up their own to the police, even if they've committed murder. The reason for this reluctance is fear of retaliation, especially if the criminal receives a light sentence and is soon back out on the streets.

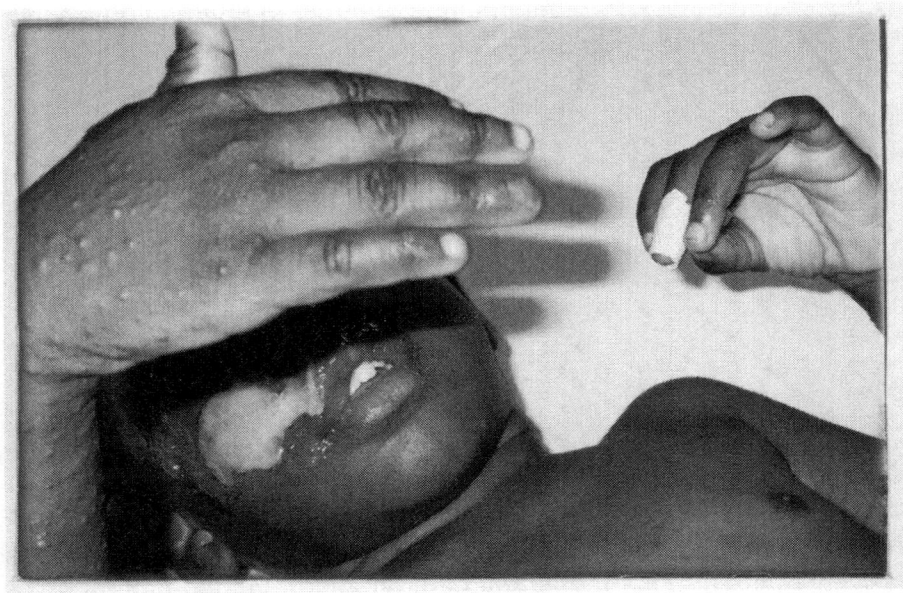

No child deserves this type of abuse. As you can see, his fingernail has been completely removed. He's been burned on his tongue and face, and he has antbites on his entire body, especially the genital area, all within 24 hours.

Detective Suzanne took the chance of showing pictures of the injuries David had inflicted on Buckey to a group of men in the projects. A short time later, David literally ran to the Police Station in fear for his life, crying, "They're trying to kill me! They're trying to kill me!" He wanted to go to jail because the men in the projects couldn't wait to get their hands on him.

Parenting Advice

Here are some tips that will help parents to form a better relationship with their infants and toddlers. Try to understand their needs, even though young children can't communicate well.

- Give consistent love and attention.
- Provide full-time supervision with a safe and caring adult.
- Teach them right from wrong.
- Recognize and encourage good behavior.
- Be a good and responsible parent or adult.
- Listen to your children.
- Look them over, especially small children.

A detective friend of mine told me that a growing trend in Child Protection Services is to give a mother a choice when a father, stepfather, or a boyfriend is accused of molesting the woman's daughter, no matter the age. That choice is either to leave the abuser or get rid of the child.

During a pregnancy a mother supposedly bonds with her child, who is helpless and dependent on the mother for her needs. Nevertheless, many mothers have said to Child Protection, "Good-bye, daughter." Yes, they choose the molesting mate over their own children. The trend is growing.

This abandonment is why so many girls are deranged and bitter and oftentimes end up choosing prostitution as a career. In many cases, Grandmothers have stepped in and try to raise their grandchildren even though they are two generations apart. The task often proves too strenuous, denying the children the firm foundation they need to succeed in life. This lack of support is the reason for most of the ill-advised choices that children make. They can't help it because they can't discern right and wrong. They have been raised in a world where there are no absolutes. Unfortunately, these poor choices often have deadly consequences, either for the child or for someone he comes in contact with.

If you are a single parent, you must act as both mother and father. I know it's hard enough working two jobs to support your children without adding the burden of double parenting, but a child needs two parents. Children need nurturing (mothering) and strong discipline (fathering). One without the other doesn't work. One without the other does not allow a child's personality to develop normally.

Being a teenager is difficult enough even when you've got all the support you need. I had both a mother and a father in my life, and still had a difficult time finding my place in life and making wise, accurate decisions. I can't imagine having only one parent in this day and age. As I look back on things, I'm sure my mother stayed with my father through the stress and strain of their marriage for us (the children). She could have chosen to leave many times, but she was forgiving and very unselfish.

Misguided Trust

Parenting is different now than what it used to be. Even the best parents can make mistakes, and one is all it takes. For instance, have you ever met someone who appeared so amiable that you and your spouse welcomed them into your home unconditionally? You develop confidence in this stranger and accord him the status of family. Yet, how much trust should you give a newcomer who seems beguiling? Should you allow him to be alone with your children? Think about these questions as you read the next case.

An East coast couple permitted a casual friend they had known less than a year to take their lovely ten-year-old daughter to a children's party. What harm can come from that? He could just drop her off at the party, and we'll pick her up afterwards, they thought. He'd shown himself to be trustworthy in the past.

"We all know him well," the parents reasoned. "We know where he lives and works. We have his phone number. He's an intelligent conversationalist with grown children and grandchildren. An established man close to retirement. What more could you ask for?"

This meek and mild older gentleman waited a year to make his move. A deviant mind will do whatever it takes to get what it wants. Instead of taking the little girl to the party, he took her to his home. She played innocently, picking flowers outside. She had long beautiful hair, a slender body, and baby blue eyes that complimented her angelic demeanor.

He then called her to come inside. At ten, she was old enough to know that something was terribly wrong because the man had taken off all his clothes. She must have been bewildered and scared when he grabbed her as she came inside the house. He quieted her screams by placing something over her mouth and held her down to strip her naked while she kicked and bit and fought him. He choked her until her sweet blue eyes rolled back into her head. Afterwards he cut her into small pieces, cooked her, and consumed her.

The family searched relentlessly after they discovered the child hadn't made it to the party. They were about to lose their minds. They wondered where they had gone wrong. What poor decisions had they made and what warning signals had they missed in their friend's behavior that had led to their daughter's disappearance? They found out after hours of investigation that their family friend used fake addresses and moved frequently. He did not return to work after the incident.

The mother and father were distraught as they waited for the neighbors or police to find their daughter. Days went by, then weeks. The suspect wrote the victim's mother a graphic letter of her daughter's last moments. He wrote that the child was a virgin, which made the sweetest meat, and, though he did not have intercourse with her, she was the sweetest meat that one could possibly eat. This sixty-five-year-old man was finally caught after intense investigation and arrested.

While being evaluated by psychologists, he told them that for years he had been sticking needles into his body, especially in his genital area between the rectum and scrotum. He used needles of all sizes, big and small. He'd done this to children as well. At first, he said he only pierced himself with the needles and then jerked them out. Gradually, he progressed to sticking them so far into his body that he was unable to retrieve some of them.

A series of X-rays and pelvic exams verified that he had twenty-nine needles inside his body, some of which had been there for at least seven years and were corroded. The family had trusted and accepted this seemingly meek, grandfather-like, sixty-five-year-old charming friend into their home because he had gained their utmost confidence and respect.

The Inner Voice

Think and then think again! Don't take the chance! Be apprehensive! Our children are our responsibility and no one else's. No matter how inconvenienced you are, put their safety first. Protecting your children is a way of showing love and concern. A feeling of apprehension is an inner signal that something is wrong with a situation. Follow your instincts.

Apprehension is what kept Raegene alive. Raegene fell in love with an ex-convict. Not all ex-convicts are perilous, but they need to be screened like any other stranger. This ex-con, for example, just couldn't shake that institutionalized lifestyle. His name was Hans.

Hans had been acting strangely for about a week according to his live-in girlfriend, Raegene. His behavior was threatening and the vibes she picked up on were so disturbing she was afraid to go home at times. Raegene wanted to break off the relationship, but she was afraid of how Hans would react. He had been known to show up where she worked when he was mad to cause trouble.

Having decided to tell Hans that she wanted to break up, Raegene decided at the last minute to stay at the house of a friend whom Hans didn't know. She had an eerie feeling that Hans knew the relationship was coming to an end and was waiting at her house to do her bodily harm. She realized there was nothing in the house worth losing her life over.

While staying that night with friends, she learned the police were looking for Hans for the murder of an eighty-three-year-old lady. Hans had hit the lady so hard that her dentures were knocked out of her mouth. Later the next day they found Hans not far from

Raegene's house. He'd been waiting for her to come home. He told police that he would have killed Raegene when she arrived. It was her apprehensiveness that warned her not to go home, or that inner voice of wisdom that guides us into all truth (John 16:13).

If you feel your mate may do you or someone else bodily harm, don't go near him or place other innocent lives in danger. Don't seek safety at a location known to him. Many people have been killed behind what I call, "Someone else's mess"! When someone gives you vibrations that just don't seem right, do what your instinct tells you. Stay away, especially if they've displayed violent tendencies before or made threats of a harmful nature.

Foolish Decisions

Imprudent decisions and foolish mistakes concerning men are not limited to the young. Older women can make serious errors in judgment as well. Have you ever heard the saying, "Two are better than one"? That's what thirty-eight-year-old Miranda thought. Others seemed to be successful at having affairs or more than one lover at a time. However, misguided in her choices, Miranda made a foolish decision.

Miranda had gone through a bitter divorce and started to play the "dating game" since it seemed as though no one in this world was faithful. She dated several men, some of whom she'd met in the local bars and others she'd met through acquaintances. Miranda formed a relationship with Paul, and they started living together about a month after they met. Then Paul's best friend, Matt, forty-one, came over, and Miranda was attracted to him.

Matt tried to withstand her come-ons, but Miranda was so compelling, Matt couldn't resist. She then started seeing Matt behind Paul's back. When Paul found out about it, he kicked Miranda out of the house and she moved in with Matt.

Matt had somewhat of a bad temper and had several brushes with the law. Not only was he hotheaded, he was also a very emotional guy. Matt tried to please Miranda with all his heart, even though arguments were common. Matt, too, was divorced, and he had never learned how to have a meaningful relationship. His ex-wife had cheated on him, and he had cheated on her. Matt had been in and out of relationships with several different women and often abused them when he became angry. Miranda never even tried to learn about Matt's background because she was so busy playing the field.

One Saturday Matt had planned to cook a nice dinner for Miranda. They had agreed to be home by 7:00 p.m. before they both left to shop and run errands. Miranda didn't come home for two days. Naturally, Matt was furious and, after she returned home, they had a brief argument and decided to split up. Matt had always suspected that Miranda was seeing someone else, but he hadn't been able to prove it. Now he became obsessed with finding out who it was.

Matt wouldn't hear from Miranda for days at a time, and then she would call him from an unknown location. If Miranda were seeing someone else, she was playing the game quite well. At least she thought she was playing it well.

Matt tried everything to try to find out who Miranda was seeing. He hinted that he would tell her boss she was on drugs unless she told him who she was seeing. She kept on playing the game unto one day Matt traced the number somehow. He asked her, "Is it true?" He'd recognized the number right away. Finally, after much denial, she confessed that it was Reginald, Matt's best friend. You know the old saying, "What goes around comes around; but when it comes back to you, it comes back in full force." Matt was devastated. He even contemplated suicide. He was confused. "How could she do that to me?" he asked himself, forgetting the pain he had caused Paul.

I Can't See the Azaleas
True Crimes Against Women and Children

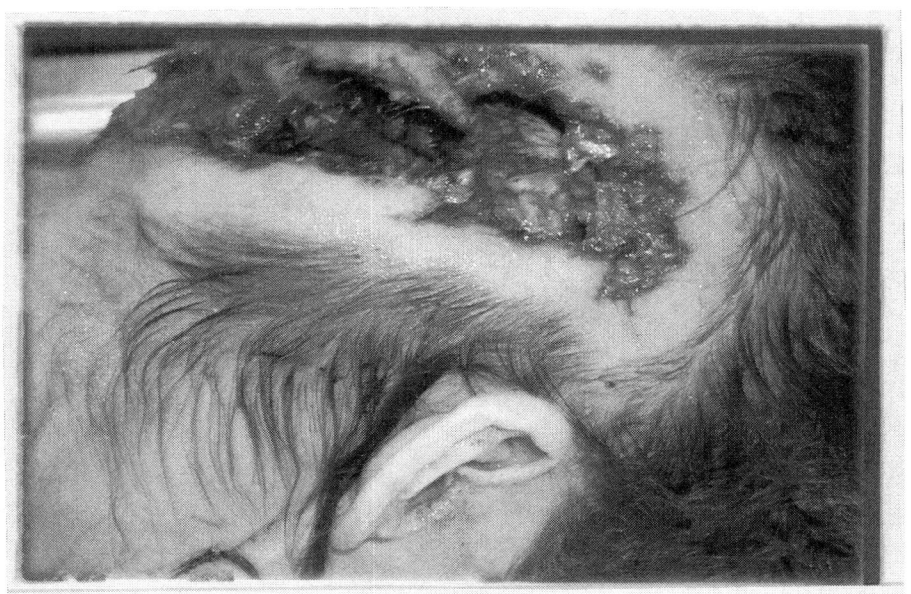

Playing games with people's lives not only ends up in domestic abuse, but possibly fatality. As she lay on the coroner's slab, her fun game came to an end.

Dianna Cook Thomas

One day Matt borrowed a friend's vehicle and drove to Reginald's house, wanting to talk the matter over and resolve it. Reginald was outside working in the yard with his mother when Matt drove up and asked, "Why haven't you returned my phone calls?"

Reginald replied, "I haven't had the time."

This wounded Matt even more because he knew where Reginald had been spending his time with Miranda. Then he asked where Miranda was, and Reginald replied, "She's up at the house."

The house sat at the end of a long, narrow driveway. Matt sped up the driveway, and Reginald and his mom heard two shots. They began to run up the driveway as Matt was driving away. Matt pulled his gun out and pointed it at Reginald, but his mother was behind him, making it impossible to shoot Reginald without harming his elderly mom, so he drove off. When Reginald found Miranda, she lay in a pool of blood with gunshots to the arm and head. She died instantly. The game was over.

Hours later the police got a call that someone had been shot. The victim was Matt. After leaving the scene of Miranda's death, Matt had tried to kill himself by pointing a gun in his mouth, but he missed and shot himself in the chest. He knew that sooner or later the police would be looking for him. They soon caught up with him, and he was arrested.

The police asked Matt several questions during the interrogation. One was, "What did you say to Miranda before you shot her?" He said, "Miranda, you're a lying whore." Matt survived his suicide attempt, and he is now serving time.

You see, playing with an individual's emotions can be deadly, not fun. Don't make the mistake that Miranda and others have made. Just because others have gotten away with it doesn't make it right.

Having multiple lovers is a dangerous game no matter how fun and exciting it may seem at the time. Having multiple partners can lead to sexually transmitted diseases, AIDS, heartbreak, broken homes, and ultimately death.

Watch for Clues

Unfortunately, sufficient clues about a man's true nature aren't always available at the beginning of a relationship. Sailing, windsurfing, pleasure boating, swimming, and waterskiing were what Jeremy did to court Jessica. The courtship lasted for a couple of years before he asked for her hand in marriage. She did marry him, and why not? Jeremy enjoyed the same pleasures in life as she did. He was loving and caring, and they enjoyed each other's company. He had an explosive temper, but she believed she could tame that in time. Both Jeremy and Jessica were polished and educated with masters' degrees and both had profitable jobs.

A year after their marriage came little Jazzman, but the couple did not adapt well to the change in their active lifestyle—the demanding responsibilities of family life. Disputes and disagreements escalated into several minor scuffles. A few seemingly trivial violent episodes would occur, leaving scrapes and abrasions, but nothing requiring medical attention. Jessica was too ashamed to call the police. What would the neighbors think?

On the night of Jeremy's birthday, the couple celebrated by having a few sips of wine. Not much, but just a little to celebrate since two-month-old Jazzman was finally asleep in his bedroom. Under the influence of alcohol, Jeremy became filled with rage. His words were hard.

After a few more sips of wine, the baby started to cry. Jessica got up to go feed him, but Jeremy angrily insisted that he would do it. He got up and went into Jazzman's room. Jessica noticed that the baby was crying forcefully as Jeremy shoved the bottle into his mouth. Jessica became furious because Jeremy was being so rough with the baby, and she took the child away and insisted that Jeremy get out. They argued as she continued to tell him to pack up and get out.

After about thirty minutes of quarreling and Jessica pacing the floor while holding the baby, Jeremy asked, "Do you really want me to leave?"

Still angry, she replied, "Yes."

Then he hit her in the face with his fist. She fell to the floor with the baby. While down on the floor he stabbed her with a letter opener.

As she kept passing in and out of consciousness, he pulled her head up and the letter opener fell out of her neck. He cut her forehead with a pocket knife as he threw her toward the door. He dragged her for a distance, leaving carpet burns on her face and body.

She remembers crawling backwards and saying, "Please don't." He kept coming in and out of the room looking for their gun. On one of his trips out of the room, she made a getaway, leaving the child behind.

Jessica was okay after numerous surgeries, and little Jazzman was fine. Jeremy was finally arrested. But life was not the same for Jessica. She was left with numerous scars on her face and body as well as a wounded spirit.

Now that she's out of that horrible marriage, Jessica has a chance to live a happy and normal life. But will she? The answer could be yes, or it could be no. With counseling and time, it could happen.

The Wrong Place To Find Love

In 1996, Sable, who was recently divorced and had a boy toddler, met Doug, who was also recently divorced, and had a girl toddler. Doug would often get his daughter and bring her over to play with Sable's boy, and they all enjoyed each other's company.

One day the couple decided to barbecue and have a few drinks. Doug and Sable each invited friends over to party in the backyard. What Sable didn't know, because it was so early in the relationship, was that Doug had a hidden secret—he was a drug user. That night Doug had a few beers and secretly smoked some crack cocaine without Sable's knowing.

While Sable was playing hostess to the guests, her son became irritated and wanted her undivided attention. He was tired from all the running and playing. So Doug, with Sable's blessing, walked the toddler to his bedroom and placed him in his bed. Doug, drunk and under the influence, tried to pacify the toddler to no avail. He wanted only his mother's attention, and Doug just wanted to go back to the company of his friends.

As the toddler continued to wail, Doug became so irritated that he hit him with enough force to propel the child across the room where he hit his head on the wall and lost consciousness. Doug hurriedly placed him in the bed on his stomach and covered him up as though he were asleep. Doug returned to his guests as though nothing had happened. After all the guests had left for the night, Doug and Sable shared an enjoyable night of lovemaking.

I Can't See the Azaleas
True Crimes Against Women and Children

The following morning, Doug did nothing out of the ordinary. He got cleaned up, cleaned up his daughter, and when Sable suggested that Doug get her son for a bath, he went to the boy's room. Doug asked Sable to come and look at the boy because he was not moving. When she saw him, he was cold and bruised. He was dead and had been for ten to twelve hours, as the investigation revealed.

What could have happened? An investigation revealed that Doug killed the baby while under the influence. What could Sable do now? It was too late to screen Doug to determine if he was on drugs or had a problem with his temper.

The Innocence of a Child

A little girl became restless as the preacher's sermon dragged on and on. Finally, she leaned over to her mother and whispered, "Mommy, if we give him the money now, will he let us go?"

This little girl didn't quite understand how church worked, but understanding comes with time. The surroundings in which you place your children can mean the difference between having the time to gain understanding and cutting your child's life tragically short.

Four-year-old Jamica was such a child. She loved doing the things most girls her age enjoy. She said cute, funny little things that only a parent could love and laugh at. She had dolls, riding toys, games, and she spent time each day getting familiar with them. Mom's new boyfriend, Art, seemed like an honest person.

When a brand-new baby came along, Jamica didn't get as much attention as before, but that was okay. Jamica liked her new sibling. Mom spent a lot of time with the new baby, and Art gave Mom lots of money, even though he didn't have a job. Art regularly brought his friends over, who liked to smoke cigarettes, drink, and laugh a lot.

The family always slept late because they stayed up late drinking and mingling. The things happening in Jamica's life were too much for her to understand, so she just went along as a four-year-old would. One day

Dianna Cook Thomas

she heard Mommy tell Art that she didn't want his new friends to come by because she didn't trust them. They argued about this like they argued about lots of things. Art refused to listen. He said he'd have around whomever he wanted.

In the early hours of a dark morning in 2001, Mommy and Art decided to go for a ride to get more beer. After leaving the local store, Jamica heard Art tell Mom, "Someone's following us."

"He sure looks familiar," Mom observed while holding the new baby in her lap. "Buckle up, Jamica, so you'll be secure," she added.

"That car is still behind us," Art acknowledged. "Oh, now they're going around us."

Suddenly the family heard, "Pow, pow, pow, pow, pow..." Screaming...squealing...and more screams from Mom.

"Oh, thank God the baby is okay," Mom cried.

"Are you okay?" Art asks Mom.

"Yes," she answered. "That's the guy you know, Art. I told you to stay away from him," Mom scolded. "At least they're gone now. Boy, that was close. Are you okay, Jamica?"

Jamica was four years old when she died from a single gunshot wound to the head. Her chances to grow and learn were over. Senseless. The company you keep may someday come back to haunt you.

Whatever Happened to "Leave It to Beaver"?

In contrast to the environment in which Jamica found herself, some people live a lifestyle patterned after "Leave It to Beaver." A conventional family setting where dinner with everyone gathered around the table is typical. Mom and Dad nurture and discipline their children and model the good ethics of the community.

At the grocery store, parents try to balance their children's likes and dislikes with the money budgeted for groceries, because neither food nor money must be wasted. Work and school come each Monday morning as you look forward to Friday and the weekend that seems to last but a second. Time passes quickly, but the routine gives a sense of permanence.

But what happens when an unanticipated upheaval due to a family separation, divorce, illness, or loss of

I Can't See the Azaleas
True Crimes Against Women and Children

income breaks this routine and your sense of security? Some people look for a quick fix to fill the empty space that togetherness and love once occupied. That's what happened to Louisiana.

Louisiana, named after the state, had it all at one time, but lost it when her spouse abandoned the family. She was left with three young mouths to feed, and they looked to her exclusively for food and shelter. Raising three children on her own had never been in her plan. Louisiana looked for answers in things which only left her empty and hollow inside.

As stress engulfed her, sleep evaded her. She became dependent on prescription drugs to get her through the night and coffee and stimulants to get her through the day. She became increasingly tolerant to the effects of the drugs, and instead of healing, the empty space inside her grew and was difficult to mask. She didn't know where to turn.

Louisiana had few close friends left. Her married friends had little time for her, and she felt that she couldn't relate to her single acquaintances whose lives seemed so much easier. In addition, it seemed her hand was always out needing to borrow a pamper or a cup of sugar, with no realistic hope that she'd be able to repay the favor. She felt no one would seriously consider a relationship with a woman with three small children. So one-night stands seemed the only way to fill her emptiness, even if it was only for a moment. Of course, these encounters only intensified the emptiness and gave her life a feeling of constant grief.

One day there was a knock on her door. Louisiana peeked through the blinds trying to be inconspicuous. On the other side were two middle-aged women in neat dresses and hats holding a "Watchtower" booklet. Oh, those Jehovah's Witnesses again, she thought to herself.

Louisiana decided to be still so they would think that no one was home. Soon, the two ladies left. Louisiana returned to her bed of melancholy. Hours turned into days, and days turned into weeks. She continued her ineffective attempts to cope. She thought, I had it made once. She reminisced about the days when she used to look out of the window during dinnertime with her family and remark how lovely and colorful the Azaleas were. Now, she didn't even notice when they came and went, or if they came at all.

Dianna Cook Thomas

Louisiana decided that she'd had enough and that it was time to party. After all, she felt she deserved it. So she got dressed, left her small children with a neighbor, and out she went. When it became a regular occurrence, the neighbor who had a family of her own got tired of having to get up in the early morning hours so Louisiana could pick up her children. The baby-sitting stopped. Still feeling the need to enjoy herself, Louisiana left her children at home by themselves when she went out because she felt she deserved some happiness. Going out to party was the only thing that relieved her despair—or so she thought.

When Louisiana's mother and father found out about the children being home alone, they came and took them. They could not stop their daughter's negligent behavior, but they could protect their grandchildren from it. There are many grandparents caring for their grandchildren because they love and cherish them. Many have come out of retirement to raise another family.

Relieved of the responsibility of her children, Louisiana was free to stay out as late as she liked, or even several nights at a time. She stayed out with all types of people just to feel (almost) gratified. Then one day there was a knock on the door. It was a male friend who seemed interested in her. It had been so long since anyone cared. The hollow hole inside felt like it was beginning to close.

After about a week of courtship, her new lover introduced her to drugs. She said no at first, but eventually she was made to choose between drugs and companionship. She chose the drugs. After all, what harm would a few drugs do? She could stop if the relationship didn't work out. She spent more and more time with her lover and the drugs, and less time with Mom, Dad, and her three children. But it didn't matter because life was better, and she could see her parents and children anytime.

Then another change came into her life. She began to see less of her new boyfriend, and she began to crave more of the drugs he used to supply for her. Her boyfriend abruptly disappeared. She drove around at night looking for him to give her more drugs and the tender love and care he once gave. She thought she could trust him. Finally, she stopped looking for him and just looked for the drugs. Louisiana became desperate. The supply of drugs she found comforted her only briefly with a high that never quite seemed to give her complete satisfaction. She was chasing a high that always seemed just out of reach.

She found herself surrounded by people who were only out for what they could get. Realizing this one day, she thought to herself, This is not me. I need to quit. She tried to get her life together with disappointing results.

The end came with a knock on the door. It was someone she knew, but not well. Both were looking to chase that high again. They drove behind a nearby church and parked. He wanted money to buy more drugs, but Louisiana didn't have any. He suggested that she pawn her jewelry, but it was the only thing she had left that still tied her to her family. They argued. She told him to get out. He asked for the jewelry again. She yelled, "No, get out."

The perpetrator took out a knife, but Louisiana couldn't believe he was going to harm her. He stabbed her several times as she struggled but it was too late. She didn't have time to scream. He threw her out of the vehicle and left. A worker found her partially nude body the next morning as he was doing his normal cleaning at the church. Louisiana would never behold the beauty of her children—never admire with them the beauty of the Azalea.

Hopeful Happiness

The next couple were a match made in heaven. The excitement of courtship led to a fairy-tale marriage ceremony followed by a honeymoon that was a dream come true. They returned from the honeymoon and moved into an exquisite apartment. They shopped for new furniture and decorated their home. They were inseparable. She never questioned their promise to be there for each other "till death do we part."

Soon exciting news arrived. Caleb was pregnant. She was cute as a button while pregnant, and Albert showed the signs of a proud dad-to-be. The labor pains seemed insignificant compared to the bundle of joy arriving soon. They relished the arrival of their new daughter, but phase two of the marriage would be challenging.

All marriages go through good times and bad. Caleb and Albert were no exception. Albert spent more time at the office as Caleb stayed home to care for the baby. Caleb began to feel that Albert was tired of the routine of marriage—the fun times seemed to be over. As the years of the routine continued, Albert was absent from the home more and more. Albert's absences weren't always because he was at work or simply out with male friends. Affairs began as did his quarreling with Caleb.

Caleb really never had a clear focus on life, and after twenty-five years of a roller-coaster marriage, she wondered if life would ever get better. To make matters worse, her mother became very ill. She felt hopeless because no one can take the place of a good and loving mother. Between an adulterous husband and a sick mother, it seemed she could easily have said, "Why me?" But instead she thought to herself, Why not me? Her mother had instilled in her the belief that she could accomplish whatever she put her mind to, including personal happiness.

As a young man, Albert had been an average looking guy. But have you ever noticed how some men become more and more handsome as they get older? That was Albert. In his fifties he had salt-and-pepper gray hair, an olive complexion, an athletic build, with beautiful eyes and soft hands. As Albert got better looking, women couldn't resist him. It didn't matter that he had a wife and daughter and that he was a church-going man.

This left Caleb and their daughter home alone most nights. Sunday morning church seemed to be their only time together. Albert occasionally stopped the affairs, especially after the tension with Caleb would explode into an argument, but soon another affair would begin.

As those heartbreaking years continued, Albert's affairs became more prominent and obvious, and Caleb seemed to get weaker and weaker. While Caleb was at one of the lowest points in her life with an adulterous husband and a sick mother, she decided to focus on getting well rather than on waiting for Albert to change his ways.

Just when she thought, Things couldn't possibly get any worse, they did. One summer day, Caleb, in her early fifties, was diagnosed with breast cancer. As she was in and out of the hospital, Albert decided to leave.

Caleb was too tired to fight for his affection this time and too weak to try. After thirty-two years of marriage, Caleb knew that arguing with Albert wouldn't do any good. She decided that if he could leave her as ill and weak as she was, it was not worth the battle of trying to save the marriage. Caleb let him go. Though she thought there was something different about this departure, she continued to focus on other matters.

Caleb felt that if she kept a strong faith she could and would recover. She couldn't worry. Concern is appropriate, but to worry causes your health to deteriorate and serves no good purpose. It doesn't solve anything. In Matthew, chapter 6, Jesus talks about the futility of worry. He says of the lilies, "Consider the lilies of the field, how they grow: they neither toil nor spin; and yet I say to you that even Solomon in all his glory was not arrayed like one of these" (vv. 28-29). Worry is debilitating and exhausting. Caleb felt if they divorced, it would be hard to find a mate at her age.

At that point, Caleb tried to bury the past and develop a sanguine attitude that drew on the power of self and the goodness of others. She came to the realization that her good health was more important than her adulterous husband and the thirty-two years she had given him. She also had to learn that happiness doesn't reside in another person or place. You are responsible for your own well-being.

Psalm 37:1-2 says, "Do not fret because of evildoers, nor be envious of the workers of iniquity. For they shall soon be cut down like the grass, and wither as the green herb."

Caleb was far from the support of close family members who all lived in the North, but she had her daughter to live for. Caleb was rich, not with money, but with benevolence. Her co-workers showed their thoughtfulness during her trips in and out of the hospital. Caleb learned to cultivate values that produced happiness. The values of goodness, kindness, mercy, fidelity, honesty, justice, loyalty, and dependability will make you rich even when your purse is empty. What gives life real value is doing something worthwhile for humankind and having something to live for.

Naturally, Caleb thought about Albert from time to time, the good times and the bad, but she had to keep looking forward. Perhaps her attitude was similar to that of Paul in the Bible: "I press toward the goal for the prize of the upward call of God in Christ Jesus"

(Philippians 3:14). Caleb had once trusted Albert, but that trust had worn away with each betrayal. She wanted their daughter to grow up with the love and support of two parents. Caleb had fought steadily by Albert's side to make their marriage work. She stayed with Albert through the agonizing days of his affairs until she couldn't hold on anymore.

By October, Albert still hadn't tried to reconcile. In the following weeks, Albert filed for a quick divorce. Caleb accepted it and prepared for a new life without Albert.

Three days after Caleb and Albert's divorce became final, he disclosed that he'd probably made a mistake. But he didn't yet realize what a tragic mistake it had been.

Albert and his lover Opal were home alone that night in 2000. Albert was spending the night since they were leaving to go on a trip the next morning. Opal's ex-boyfriend Sam, broke into her house while both were naked and in bed asleep. Sam shot Albert once in the head. He shot Opal once in the head, then turned the gun on himself. All three died instantly. When Caleb found out about it, she was stunned. Only a few months had passed since Albert left.

When the police arrived at the scene, they too looked in disbelief at the bloodbath of the crime scene. Caleb now had to come to the realization that Albert was finally and truly gone. Caleb is now physically well, but she is still hurting emotionally after the death of Albert. Caleb has learned that life is too short to waste on wrong decisions. The temptations Albert faced are common, but God's Word promises with every temptation He will make a way of escape (1 Corinthians 10:13).

During Christmas 2001, Caleb received a bracelet as a gift from her daughter. It was engraved, "My hero, my friend." It was a special moment created out of the love that helped keep Caleb strong.

Soon after Albert's death, Caleb's mom was hospitalized with cancer. She was in her last stages. Caleb's heart was broken as she took a flight North to find her mom lying on her deathbed. The tears streamed down her face as she tried with all of her might to fight them back. She didn't want to let her mom see how fragile and grieved she was. Her mother died a few days later.

Caleb was gaunt from grief. She knew that she must go on, but how? It was hard to lose her mother, especially when she supported her through all her disappointments. Caleb remembered her mom's voice so sweet and strong, saying, "You can do it. You can do it" just as she had when Caleb felt she was too weak to turn her mom over in her hospital bed.

You too can do it. Just like Caleb who slowly but determinedly convalesced. When people asked her, "How are you today, Caleb?" at first her reply was, "Okay." Then it became, "Fine." Then, "Good." She even has some "great" days now, but there are those "fine" days that burden her from time to time. It's a gradual process, but we can never get better without trying. Improvement in our lives doesn't come magically, effortlessly, or without setbacks. Struggles come periodically into every life, but triumphant people don't give up. They don't stay fainthearted for long. They are not quitters, and when they encounter a setback, they face it and keep moving forward.

I admire Caleb. She's so normal, strong, and faithful. She reminds me of my favorite Aunt Luverdia who is quiet, mild-mannered, and meek. She has a strong desire, that comes from the goodness of her heart, to help others. She put me back on the right track when I seemed to be going astray. It's as if God left an angel to guard over us when He took my mother to heaven. My mother is an angel in heaven, and I'm blessed with an angel right here on earth.

Caleb walks life in faith with friends who are dear to her. That has kept her going. Some people never ascend to the higher ground because they've never seen the mountain peak. They languish in the dry and constricting valley below. There are great advancements and attainments, lucrative possibilities, and glorious opportunities that arise, but they don't exist for those who don't have the vision to discern them.

Caleb's greatest accomplishment was learning how to profit from her experiences, both good and bad. Your past experiences can be either hurtful or helpful, depending on the use you make of them. If you brood over them, they're unproductive and useless. If you learn from them and use that knowledge to build a firm foundation, you can turn them into the basis for higher achievements.

Forgiveness Is the Key

Caleb also learned to forgive. If you have been mistreated in the past and can't forgive and move on, it poisons your present. But if you let go and forgive, you can live today free and ready to do what's necessary to keep going.
The Word of God declares:

> "And whenever you stand praying, if you have anything against anyone, forgive him, that your Father in heaven may also forgive you your trespasses.
> "But if you do not forgive, neither will your Father in heaven forgive your trespasses."

Mark 11:25-26

In John 20:23 Jesus says, "If you forgive the sins of any, they are forgiven then; if you retain the sins of any, they are retained."
Caleb moved to another house and attends a different church than the one she and Albert attended. She hopes to have companionship one day. Remember, life is like the Azalea blossom, here today and gone tomorrow. While you have it, treasure it. While you are here, live right, treat others with benevolence and respect. Keep the faith in times of struggle because one day it will fade away, just like an Azalea blossom.
I can relate to Caleb because I've been through it myself. Dating was so much fun, and the marriage ceremony was beautiful. Moving into a new apartment with a fireplace and new furniture gave a sense of permanence to our unity. I felt as though all my dreams had come true.
Then, reality set in. Trying to please my husband wasn't doing any good because I began to see less and less of him. "What am I doing that would make him not want to stay home with me?" I'd ask myself. I tried to look as perfect as I could and do things as perfectly as could be just to please him. I even wore makeup and perfume to bed so I would always look beautiful for him.

I Can't See the Azaleas
True Crimes Against Women and Children

No matter how hard I tried, nothing seemed to work. After three agonizing years, I found out why. He had another woman in his life. When I finally saw her, I was floored. She was not attractive at all. There were times when I saw my husband so little that I'd ask him to marry her and come to visit me!

Looking back on those years of trials and tribulations, I can see why it happened. I learned something positive from it all. It was exhausting trying to please him while getting zero results. I now realize that I put too much effort into pleasing my husband.

Now, I do what it takes to please God first, then my family and me second. Sometimes I wear my natural hair, but I may wear weaves, wigs, or extensions, whatever pleases me on a particular day. My husband asked me one day, "What in the hell do you have on your head now?"

I told him, "If I wear a bird's nest on my head with the bird still in it, it's nobody's business but mine. And besides, I'd look better in it than any woman you had an affair with on her best day."

On another day I wore my wig, a scarf, and a hat on my head just to go shopping. I thought it was rather cute. My husband asked me, "Why in the hell do you have all this stuff on your head?"

I shot back, "When you were busy having your affairs, you wouldn't have cared if I'd tied a motorcycle around my head, so what makes it any different now?" He knew that he'd better leave me alone. He couldn't say a thing. He knew better than to get me started because when I shake my head and snap my finger like a true black woman, the case is closed.

No one wants to go through what Caleb and I experienced because it hurts. It's depressing and there were a lot of sleepless nights filled with tears, but it made me realize I needed to do a lot of growing myself. A lot of self-evaluation took place. It took that tribulation to make me look within. When I examined my motives, habits, words, and deeds, I was able to grow in character with God's help.

Events that are negative can be used positively. I found that out. By looking at where I had succeeded and where I had failed determined if I had done my best. It changed my whole view on life. As I took that self-inventory, I realized life is short and can become self-destructive if it goes unexamined.

Paul said, "Examine yourselves as to whether you are in the faith. Test yourselves..." (2 Corinthians 13:5).

Chapter 11

I Have a Financially Secure Future

    Warm breezes flowing through shady trees and a special kind of peace that comes with nature are all a part of living your golden years. A home neighboring a recreation area can provide a relaxing and gratifying environment for any elderly couple wishing to spend their retirement years surrounded by natural beauty. This is the kind of life many of us long to experience in our retirement years.
    Unfortunately, something in this plan went terribly wrong for Helen. The death of her husband and deteriorating health left her in the care for her forty-eight-year-old son, John.
    Helen's health declined slowly as the years passed. Helen's neighbors did not see her over the winter months of her final year. John was so unapproachable, neighbors were afraid to consult him about her welfare.
    As spring approached, the Azaleas were ready to bloom, and everything seemed to be going well. There were still some very cold days and nights, but the harsh winter months were past. One March day John asked one

of his mother's neighbors to help him load her in a vehicle to take her to the hospital due to illness.

"Sure," acknowledged the neighbor. "Not a problem."

The neighbor expected he would help support Helen as they walked to the car and then help her into the front seat. When the neighbor walked into the house he was shocked. The house was filthy and filled with a foul odor, and Helen was lying on the floor on a mat near the bathroom. The smell and the appearance of Helen were shocking. She appeared to be alive, but scarcely.

"Why don't you call EMS?" the neighbor asked.

"Oh, I don't trust those people. I'll just take her myself," replied John.

So the neighbor helped get Helen to the pickup truck where, instead of putting her in the front seat, John placed her in the bed of his truck. The truck had a camper shell on the back, but there wasn't a back door, and it was nippy outside. As a matter of fact, that particular March day was exceptionally cold and windy.

When John arrived at the hospital with Helen, her body temperature was 85 degrees. She was unconscious and unresponsive. She was half nude and swaddled in a blanket. Helen died twenty minutes after arriving at the hospital.

Suspicious Circumstances

The hospital staff called the police because they knew the signs of neglect in the elderly. Helen was definitely a victim. She had obviously been neglected and must have weighed only 80 pounds.

When detectives arrived, the doctor explained that Helen had died of hypothermia due to neglect and malnutrition. She had large sores on her thighs, and her skin was light and irritated on both of her legs. According to the doctor, the reason the sores were open, irritated, and red was probably due to lying in urine for an extended period of time. The malnutrition was due to lack of feeding.

John told the doctors that Helen had suffered a light stroke years before and required a walker to get around. He stated his mother's health had been deteriorating since the stroke. He said that lately he'd noticed her face and feet were swollen. He thought it was some type of allergic reaction to something she ate.

I Can't See the Azaleas
True Crimes Against Women and Children

John further stated that his mother had been living on a cot in the bathroom and that he had to assist her since she couldn't make it to the toilet on her own. John told doctors he'd also observed discoloration on her feet. He felt his mother had contracted some type of disease, but he was incapable of taking her anywhere because he had no money for gas for his truck or anything else. John stated that he did not trust the EMS. He said that he had his neighbor help him load his mother into the back of the truck and claimed, "I have him as my witness that she was still alive, you know. She was still kicking when we left home."

The detectives went out the next day to visit John at his residence. First, they interviewed neighbors and one informed them John had not let his mother receive company or leave the house in approximately two years. Another neighbor stated that she had not seen Helen in years. The detectives went to John's house last.

When John let them in, they noticed that every room was filled with garbage from the floor to the ceiling. Narrow trails led from room to room, and there was so much trash in each room that it was difficult to tell which room of the house they were in. The kitchen was a filthy mess and so was the bathroom.

In Helen's room there was a thin mat on the floor near the bathroom door. Her mat had a sheet on it, and both the sheet and the mat were saturated with urine. The smell in the room was so bad it almost made them regurgitate. There were no medicine bottles belonging to Helen anywhere in the house, suggesting that she had not been under a doctor's care, in spite of her failing health. The house had cold running water, but not hot because the hot water heater had gone out two years before, and John never had it repaired. There was no heat in the house and hadn't been for three years.

Helen didn't die a violent death, but it was an agonizing one. After the death of her husband, her life was placed in the hands of the person she should have been able to trust the most. The one who, as a child, she had given a warm bed to sleep in, good clothing, and a safe environment. He was given nutritional food and the care of a physician when needed. She gave all she had, but gained nothing in return. If only Helen could have sought advice early on, or if she could have reached out to someone, maybe things would have turned out differently.

Dianna Cook Thomas

Helen should never have spent her golden years in this fashion. I'm sure she thought she would be financially secure and physically able to care for herself in her golden years. As a younger woman, Helen, like many of us, assumed she would be financially independent and in good physical and mental health throughout her life. She imagined an old age shared with her husband, son, and grandchildren in peaceful surroundings. A tranquil setting filled with beautiful Azaleas in the spring. Instead, her life was broken by her failing health and the mental illness of her son. Perhaps financial planning on her part and intervention by others could have prevented this tragedy.

I Can't See the Azaleas
True Crimes Against Women and Children

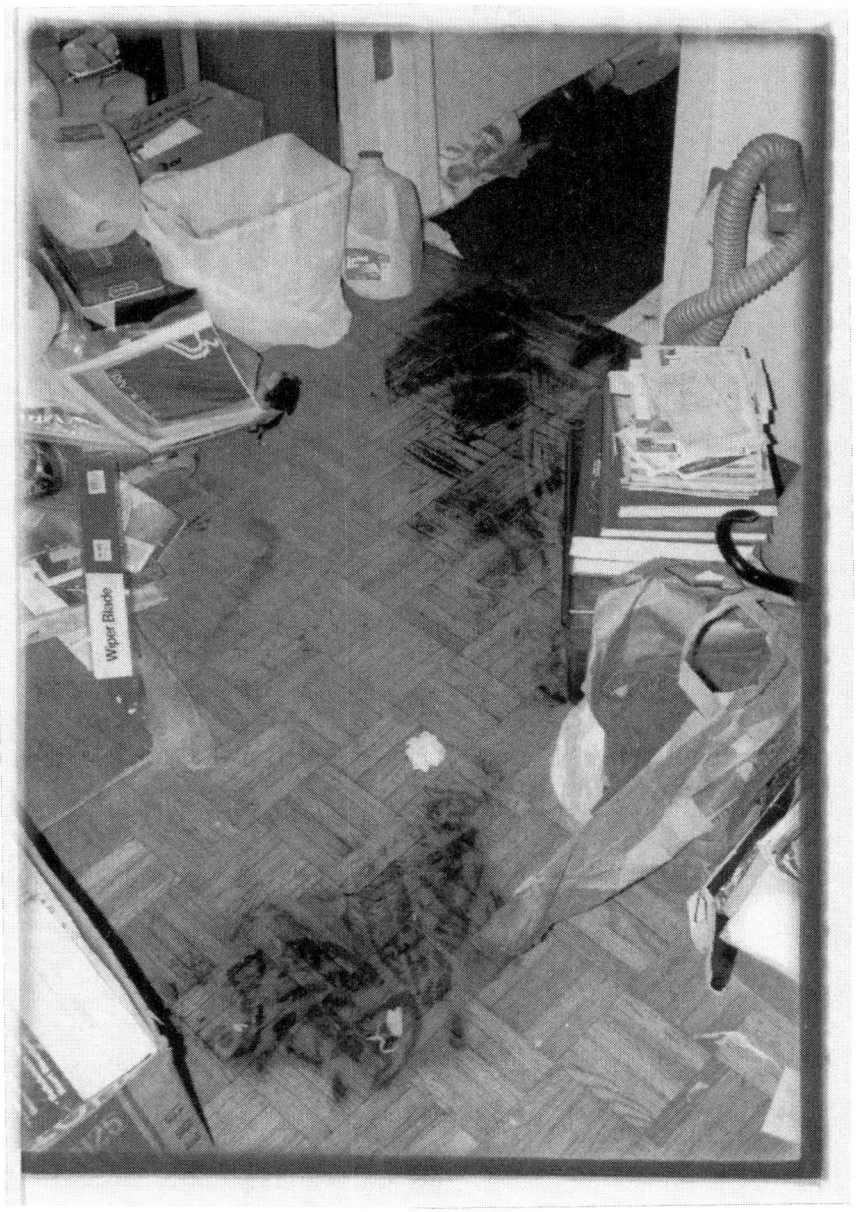

The elderly shouldn't have to tolerate this kind of abuse in their golden years...especially from their own children.

Dianna Cook Thomas

Gloria's Story

    It is not unusual for older women with restricted incomes to become isolated. Women like Gloria, who lived alone and survived on a small income from her husband's retirement. She had few close friends. Her family lived far away. Gloria attended services at a local church every Sunday, and she went to the local bank and grocery store once a month. She could afford no other entertainment because the money just wasn't there. She also couldn't afford to properly secure her home. She couldn't afford an extra lock on the door because food and medicine were necessities. But she was content in her solitude and didn't mind staying home most of the time.

    One particular Sunday, Gloria attended church and returned home to find a burglar in her house. Getting in was easy because there weren't any safety locks on the doors. He robbed and raped her. Afterwards, he killed her. Her body wasn't discovered until she failed to show up at church the following Sunday. It was a week before anyone missed her. This is a form of neglect, lack of concern from relatives.

    Check on elderly relatives. Call often to say hello, or have neighbors check on them periodically. Give your phone number to a trusted neighbor in case of an emergency. Have them call you if they haven't seen your elderly relative in a day or two. These tips could save a life, and it could be the life of your relative.

    Helen and Gloria never thought that financial difficulty or lack of care would plague them, not in their wildest dreams. Financial planning for retirement is not an option anymore. We're living longer, and families can't afford the cost of caring for an elderly relative. We're healthier and making more money than our parents and grandparents did, but we're spending more too. Start preparing for your retirement now. Take responsibility for your future.

If you think an elderly woman would never be raped...THINK AGAIN! She was not financially able to buy extra locks for the doors of her house because she had a small set income.

Chapter 12

I'm Too Old

> My hair was thin and yellow,
> and I asked, "What should I do?"
> My husband suggested the beauty shop,
> but then it came out blue!

The golden years should be relaxing. Grandchildren come and go. They don't stay long enough to get on your nerves, just long enough to be held and loved. I remember Grandma as someone who was always baking and cooking. She held ideas that to me seemed old-fashioned and outdated. If only I had known then what I know now. She was so full of wisdom, the kind I could have assimilated and patterned my life after. Grandma could feed everyone in the neighborhood with one modest low-budget dish. A person just had to knock on the door and say, "I'm hungry. What are you cooking today?"

Grandma, times have changed! You can't do that anymore. In this day and age, you have to yell through the door, "Go to the Mission!" If only this next elderly lady had yelled through the door, she might still be living.

There was a knock on the door. A handsome, young, white male, with a businesslike appearance, was on the other side. In his mind he was acting out his fantasies and planning to do harm. In the blue-haired lady's mind, she was imagining that this fellow had some business to conduct or wanted a drink of water. He's too nice looking to harm a little old lady like me, she thought. Sex was the furthest thing from her mind. After all, he would be interested in an attractive young girl with a figure eight, not someone in her seventies with a figure zero. She opened the door to see what he wanted. He talked his way inside, though he could just as easily overpowered her and closed the door behind him. Either way, it was too late.

This dashing man left her lying on her back completely exposed for police to find. The first thing officers saw when they entered the residence was the victim's private parts, just as her attacker had planned. There was evidence of torture to the victim. Her legs were spread about four to five feet apart and propped up on two separate chairs like at the OB-GYN clinic. She had been strangled, and although she had not been raped, she had been sexually assaulted with some type of object.

There had not been a struggle because everything was in its proper place. Elderly victims are usually weak, often feeble. The first mistake she made was thinking no one would hurt an elderly lady. The second was allowing the perpetrator inside the residence without knowing anything about him.

I teach a course to very young children called Stranger Danger. The first thing they learn is, never let a stranger into their home or get into the car with a stranger. The same rule applies to you. Looks can be deceiving, so don't get caught up with outward appearances. Considering these simple rules could have saved this woman's life.

Crimes don't happen only at night. A great many of them happen in the daytime, the same time when the elderly are most likely to run errands. Attacks can take place in your own home as well as out in public.

I Can't See the Azaleas
True Crimes Against Women and Children

Madelyn's Story

The next story concerns a suspect whose initial intent was to burglarize the home of a middle-aged female. Finding the victim there alone, however, he decided to torment her.

An exquisite petite, divorced, church-going lady in her middle fifties with an admiration for opera lived alone in a quiet, old-fashioned neighborhood. Her name was Madelyn. The burglar noticed that Madelyn was alone and could not resist the enchantment of her slim and dainty body. When her only son's attempts to contact her by phone failed, he went by her house. It was immediately apparent that the house had been broken into, but something made him uneasy.

Madelyn's son entered the house and yelled for his mom, but she didn't answer. He searched for her thinking perhaps she had run a quick errand before their lunch date. When he came to the bathroom, he noticed her silhouette on the floor. He saw the contour of his dear mother there on the floor. Her body was posed in a grotesque manner. She was naked and was placed on her hands and knees. She had been strangled and showed signs of sexual assault with an unidentified object.

Madelyn's house was easy for a would-be criminal to enter. A female who lives alone is the perfect target for a criminal. You can decrease your vulnerability by examining your surroundings. Take every precaution when leaving and entering your home alone.

Burglarproof Your Home

Is your house burglarproof? Lock all your keys in your house. Then try to gain entry. Get your son or nephew or another male you trust to help you. Could a window be broken without drawing attention, or simply raised to allow entry? Check to see if the doors are secure. Discover what it would take to get inside and get your keys.

If you can get inside easily, so can a criminal. Take away the easy access that would allow a criminal to enter your home. Secure your house with extra locks and trim your trees and bushes. A woman living alone should have no windowpane doors, or just one simple door knob.

Deadbolts and additional locks are a must. Doors should be tightly secured, and windows should be locked at all times, especially those in the rear of the house. Criminals don't like lights. Make sure your property is well illuminated. Burglars often avoid a well lit home.

    Older women tend to believe all rape victims are young, attractive women. But some rapists exclusively select the elderly. Some perpetrators will even rape a dead body (necrophilia). Don't allow your home to be too accessible. Check all windows and doors to make sure they are secure. It is always better to be safe than sorry.

    A sixty-five-year-old lady who lived alone made some of the same mistakes as others. She let a stranger into her home. He was well-groomed and had straight teeth so she trusted him. She had no strength to fight and didn't know how even if she'd had the strength. He acted out of his brutal fantasies. Her vagina and anus had been lacerated. She was found posed face down, nude, on her bed with her legs spread apart. You cannot judge a man's character by his appearance.

    There are perverted human beings who often have committed the same types of crime. They have an overwhelming urge to act out their fantasies and they do so. They live in a different world from the average citizen.

    At eighty-eight years old, a woman doesn't want to think about such perversions. This lady was doodling around her house one wintry February. She had things she wanted to clean up, after having the family for a long holiday visit. All she wanted to do was work around the house a bit. Someone broke into her easily accessible home, put a knife to her throat, and forced her to do unthinkable things. Then he raped her. When the police arrived, she couldn't even remember how the perpetrator looked because she was too traumatized and had some memory loss.

    Family members should check the residences of elderly neighbors, grandmas, moms, aunts, or even sisters and daughters to make sure their homes are secure. Check their houses to see if you can force your way in. Have an extra key made in case of an emergency. Help devise an escape plan in case of an attack.

    Wouldn't it trouble you if someone raped your mother or grandmother? Could you live with yourself knowing there was something you could have done? Don't allow

I Can't See the Azaleas
True Crimes Against Women and Children

someone to crush that fragile blossom. Safeguard them. They deserve it. It doesn't matter if you live miles away, check on their home and safety regularly.

Chapter 13

Profiling

A professional profiler uses evidence gathered by examining crime scenes or photographs to identify probable traits and characteristics of the criminal(s) involved. These professionals apply their training in specific areas of crime and human nature to the evidence and circumstances of the crime to create profiles that allow law enforcement agencies to narrow their investigations. They also help the jurors at a trial understand the dynamics of a serial killing, serial killers, and the fantasies that motivate them. A professional profiler, however, cannot look at a person and tell if they're a criminal. Neither can you.

Assuming that someone is a criminal based on race, social or economic class, level of education, appearance, or any other category is not professional profiling—it's stereotyping. Not all unclean men with scraggly hair and a beard are criminals. Not all young black men with gold teeth and saggy pants are your enemy. Not all overweight white males with a slightly balding head and thick-rimmed glasses are serial killers or rapists.

Dianna Cook Thomas

If Ted Bundy were alive today and knocked on your door, and you didn't know who he was, you'd probably let him in. Every person who knocks on your door claiming to have a legitimate reason to enter your house should have his story verified by you making one simple phone call. If you let him in without checking his story, you may become a statistic. Take the extra time to call his company and be safe.

Don't Stereotype

As a police officer, I supervised a crew of prisoners for community service detail for three years. I picked up misdemeanor prisoners, mostly males, but also a few females. I'd ask what crime they had committed, and their response for the most part was shoplifting. On one particular day I had seven black women prisoners and one white.

The white prisoner told me that in large department stores, black customers are watched so closely that she could steal the stores blind, and she often did. She found that most stores were that way. She said she was seldom watched or harassed. She had gotten caught only because of her own negligence.

Criminals use stereotyping to their advantage. Of course, some blacks do steal, but so do whites, rich people, Hispanics, Orientals, Cubans, Russians, and Germans. Some poor people steal, but an abundance of them do not. Stereotyping doesn't keep you safe from crime. It's just another device criminals use to catch you off guard. Watching out for certain types of people won't protect you. You can be deceived every time. Be cautious of everyone and everything.

We have to stop judging people by their looks. We should keep everyone at a distance until we've had a chance to make a safe evaluation. Sometimes we women think good-looking men are harmless. That's how Ted Bundy got women to let him into their homes. Most criminals are smart and can make it hard for the police to find clues to solve a crime and catch them.

We women have to take responsibility for our safety and be smart and cautious, even if it makes us feel silly at first. Killers don't know how to feel sorry for someone or how to have a normal relationship. They can be very clever and manipulating. You can claim protection from Psalm 91:11: "For He shall give His angels charge over you, to keep you in all your ways." Always ask the Holy Spirit for guidance. "However, when He, the Spirit of truth, has come, He will guide you into all truth..." (John 16:13).

It is so important to be a little suspicious of everyone, even women, because they can be part of the trap. Predators lurk in malls, churches, grocery stores, and gas stations. They might dress like an attorney, a doctor, a policeman, or even a clown. They know how to stalk their prey. They are professionals at what they do. That's why it's important to be professional at what you do, and that means being cautious.

Strange Criminal Minds

Some killers love authority and domination. They'll ask their victims, "How does it feel knowing you're going to die?" They love to torture and then resuscitate victims just to torture them all over again before they allow their victim to die. Some killers hate women with brown eyes. Others hate women who remind them of an old girlfriend they broke up with years ago. Some hate all women. Some rapists have amiable and loving wives who know nothing about their husbands' perversions as they dominate and rape innocent victims outside of their marriage. Some even have young daughters the age of their victims. Other killers have no motive other than the exhilaration murder gives them.

Four Types of Killers

I will briefly describe four types of killers: psychopaths, sociopaths, organized, and disorganized killers.

1. The psychopath - The psychopath is antisocial, aggressive, and has a highly impulsive personality. This individual feels little or no guilt about his antisocial behavior, and he just can't seem to build lasting relationships with either males or females. He has a severe mental

or personality disorder and lacks the ability to feel guilt or empathize with others.
2. The sociopath - The sociopath's behavior is solely directed toward self-fulfillment, even at the expense of other people and their safety. He has probably come into contact with law enforcement due to his inability to live by the rules and regulations of society. He only cares about his own thoughts or feelings and doesn't feel regret.
3. The organized killer - The organized killer is very hard to spot. He is neat and organized in everything he does. His need for cleanliness, order, and neatness extends to his car, job, home, and personal appearance. He is non-sociable because he chooses to be, not because others exclude him. He goes to restaurants alone, sees movies alone, and goes shopping alone. Apart from killing, his existence is rather mundane!
4. The unorganized killer - The unorganized killer is strange and bizarre. You can spot him a mile away. He moves frequently but usually stays within the same neighborhood. He typically returns to the scenes of the crimes. He'll change jobs after he kills, but he doesn't move far from the previous job. His attacks are instinctive and unpremeditated because he is unable to control his homicidal urges. After he kills, he disfigures the face of the victim and mutilates the body, often removing the genitalia, which he may take with him. He overkills by delivering numerous chops to the head and multiple slashes to the body.

These four types of killers are not your typical killers, however. They have a distinct interest in violence and may display such acts as cannibalism, necrophilia, erotic asphyxiation, and piquatism (to provoke or arouse). Some can be spotted with the naked eye and some can't. That's why vigilance is important.

The Average Victim

Seventy percent of women and children who are murdered are killed by someone they know, according to Mark Rogers, a twenty-year Crime Scene Analyst. Mark has investigated over a thousand deaths of all kinds, including serial, natural, and equivocal (the cause of death isn't immediately clear). Of all women murdered, 70 percent knew their killers.

According to Mark, "Most of the time murder is an emotional crime, and therefore victims know the person who kills them." He also says that we could increase our safety dramatically by simply refusing to put ourselves in precarious or adventurous predicaments. The number of cases in which a victim could have done absolutely nothing to improve her chances for survival are small. Be wise and listen to that still, small voice inside.

Ted Bundy was good-looking, even cute, and appeared innocent and inoffensive. He had straight teeth and was a make-believe law student. He used his appearance and demeanor to lure women. He often kept his arm in a sling to appear less threatening. Women would approach him to help him with his groceries only to find themselves abducted, raped, and beaten to death.

Don't be fooled by looks and possessions. Look deeper and make sure that an individual's actions and professed beliefs match—make sure the talk matches the walk. Listen to your innermost feelings. Be patient and give yourself the time to develop your instinct. In the church that I attend, we have a saying, "Stand still until His will is clear." In other words, stand still until you can sense what direction to choose, and you'll have a better chance of heading down the right path.

Most of the situations I've described were avoidable. The women involved in them simply made some bad choices. Listen and learn so you'll have a long life in which to enjoy the Azaleas!

Chapter 14

Crime Prevention

Being aware of crime can prevent it. Women can never have too much safety training because their life may depend on it. Here are some general safety tips. The number one security hazard is apathy. Train yourself to be alert and aware at all times.

Home

Get to know your neighbors. Check on each other regularly. Report suspicious activity in your neighborhood. Let a trusted neighbor or friend as well as the police know when you will be away so they can keep an eye on your house for you. They should also keep an eye on you in general.

Implement common sense security provisions at home when you're going to be gone. Have lights on a timer or leave lights on in different parts of the house. Leave a TV or radio on a talk show. Stop deliveries of newspapers and mail or have someone pick them up for you. Leave things looking as normal as possible.

Dianna Cook Thomas

Lock Up! Light Up!

    Lock up! Light up! Criminals do not like light. You can't burglarproof your home, but you can make it burglar resistant.
    If someone comes to your door, ask for identification before you let them in. If it is a service person you are not expecting, look up the number of the business and call for verification.
    Don't name tag your keys. Leave an extra set with a friend or relative. Don't hide them in a safe place around your home. Engrave your driver's license number on valuables. If you think someone has broken into your home while you were away, don't go in. Call the police from a neighbor's house. Let the police go in and check the house for you.

Personal

    Don't keep large sums of cash in your wallet or at home. Carry only necessary cash, especially around holidays. That's why robberies pick up during the holidays. Carry your purse under your arm, close to the body. Men should not carry their wallets in a back pocket or anywhere else they can be easily pickpocketed. Walk confidently with your head up and make eye contact. Let people know that you see them.
    Shop during the day if possible. Do not go out alone at night. Don't carry more packages than you can handle and be sure you can see over them.
    When shopping, place purchases in the trunk of your car. If your vehicle does not have a trunk, make a special trip home to drop off your purchases. Sit near the driver when using public transportation. If someone demands your wallet or purse, hand it over. Your life is more important than your money.
    Reaching out to men to change their beliefs and attitudes that permit abusive behavior needs to be a professional and community-based strategy. Ending physical and sexual violence will require long-term commitment and strategies involving all parts of society. Many governments have committed themselves to

overcoming violence against women by passing and enforcing laws that ensure women their legal rights and punish abusers.

Vehicle

When out after dark, park in a well-lighted area. Don't leave valuables visible inside your car. Keep your vehicle well-maintained with a full tank of gas. Keep windows up and doors locked, even if you are only going for a short drive or getting out for just a "minute." Don't leave your keys in the car. Lock all the doors when you park.

Keep your dome light working. Use locking gas caps. Know your license plate number and pertinent data about your car. Have your keys in your hand and glance under your vehicle as you approach it. Glance inside before unlocking it. If you think you are being followed, drive to a safe place—the police station or a store that is open. Do not panic, and do not lead someone to your home.

If you have car trouble and are stranded, put your flashers on and your hood up. Keep windows up and doors locked. If a stranger approaches, roll your window down just enough to tell the person to call for assistance. Place a placard indicating you need help where it can be seen by passing motorists.

Doors, Door Frames, and Door Locks

Solid core doors are preferable to panel doors. Thin panel or hollow core doors should be lined with metal. Glass panels should be covered with wire mesh on the inside. Doors with glass within the reach of the lock should have keyed locks on both inside and outside. Exterior doors should have non-removable hinge pins. If the door frame is weak, a lock should be used that does not depend on the frame for mounting.

Door locks should have a deadbolt feature with pick resistant cylinder. Padlocks should be of pick resistant quality with a hardened shackle. All identification numbers should be removed before installing the lock. Overhead doors should be locked either by electric power or slide bolts and/or pick resistant cylinder locks.

Windows

Sliding windows can be secured by auxiliary keyed deadbolts. Vertical and horizontal windows should be pinned with a hardened steel pin, large nail, or wooden dowel. Additional security can be acquired by cutting wooden doors to fit the grooves next to the window guides. They can be cut to the exact length of the guide to prevent the window from being opened or the dowel being removed by vibration of the window.

Lighting

Interior lights should be placed on timers to go on at various times in different rooms to give the impression at all times that someone is home. Exterior lights should be dusk to dawn or motion sensor type to eliminate places where potential burglars can conceal themselves in darkness.
Periodically check all exterior lighting to ensure that it is in good working order. Replace any burned out bulbs, elements, or fixtures.

Weaknesses and Possible Remedies

Poor visibility for neighbors or from the street to see potential burglars, allowing the burglar more time to spend attempting to get into your house is a weakness. Cut back shrubbery which may hamper people's view. Secure entrances (doors and windows) with the strongest possible locks. Poor lighting hinders a person on the street from seeing a burglar attempting to enter your home and allows the burglar more time to spend getting into your house.
Keep a light on over the entrances of your home when you are not at home as well as when you are. You don't want to signal that you aren't home by only turning lights on when you are away.

I Can't See the Azaleas
True Crimes Against Women and Children

Your home looks unoccupied when lights are not on in the home. Have a neighbor keep a key and turn lights on and off for you. Buy a timer and set your lights to come on and go off as if you were home. Get a house sitter.

Your home looks unoccupied when your lawn is overgrown. Mow before you leave or have a neighbor mow your lawn while you are away.

Your Family

No one is safe from acts of violence these days. The most dangerous kinds of street crimes are occurring in greater numbers in more places. It doesn't just happen in big city streets or in the suburbs. It also takes place in small villages, towns, and even in rural areas. The best protection is to avoid situations which prompt this kind of crime. Follow these simple precautions. Discuss them with your family. The time it takes may be the best investment you have ever made. Here are some supplementary safety precautions.

Avoid High Crime Areas

This is especially true in cities. It may seem obvious, but it bears repeating. Whenever possible, select travel routes that avoid these areas.

Be Especially Cautious at Night

Street criminals use darkness as a shield. Park your car in a well-lighted area. Don't walk down desolate streets if you don't have to. Take a cab instead.

Know Your Route Home

Know the locations of stores/businesses that are open late and the location of police and fire stations. Avoid alleys, dark parking lots, and parks.

Never Open Your Door to Strangers

Install a peephole or a wide-angle viewer. Don't be afraid to demand proper identification before opening the door for anyone.

Know What Neighbors You Can Count On

Keep a list of their phone numbers. Know their work schedule so you can keep a watchful eye out for them as well.

If You Live Alone, Don't Advertise It

Single women should list their name in the phone directory with first and middle initials; i.e., J. A. Green instead of June A. Green.

If Attacked, Shout "Fire"—Not "Help" or "Rape"

This elicits a better response. Some women carry a whistle. A shrill whistle blast can unnerve an attacker and attract attention.

When Confronted—Cooperate

Street criminals are not always rational. They may be under the influence of drugs. Do what they say and do it quickly. If a robber displays a weapon, consider it loaded. Your objective is to avoid physical injury. Get the best physical description you can and report it to the police. Most of all, try not to get into a situation where you will have to negotiate.

Children

Help your children help themselves by discussing the few simple but meaningful rules that can protect them from harm. Remind them that a policeman is a friend. Don't be afraid to talk to police officers and answer their questions. Never obey a stranger who tries to get you to enter his/her car. Don't take money or candy or gifts from strangers on the street. When a strange person drives up and asks you for directions, keep a safe distance away from his/her car when you answer. It's okay to say, "I don't know," even if you do. Just keep walking and walk fast.

Always learn the names and telephone numbers of your friends so that your parents can call them if necessary.

Don't play alone in alleys or near empty or deserted buildings. Tell your teacher or a police officer about any big person who keeps hanging around your schoolyard or follows you to or from school.

Tell your teacher or a police officer about any big person whom you don't know who wants to join in your play.

Remember to write down the license number of the car of any stranger who takes one of your friends for a ride. Use a crayon or stone to write the number on the sidewalk, or scratch it in the dirt with a stick.

Don't go into any building or rooms for any reason with a big person you don't know. Report to your teacher or a police officer any person who touches you in a way that makes you feel unpleasant or hurts you.

Preventing Violence in Children

Parents, if we raise our children around violence, they will be violent when they grow up. Here are some activities that you may not realize can lead to a house full of monsters:

TV Violence

TV violence is portrayed in many programs that seem harmless, such as the news and even cartoons. Notice if programs exhibit sexual innuendos or excessive noise. Avoid and discourage any aggressive/violent activities and behavior.

Dianna Cook Thomas

Limit Media Violence

Be a good role model. Children imitate adult behaviors, no matter how insignificant. Monitor children's behavior after watching certain shows or videos. Even after they finish with the computer, look for signs of unusual behaviors and activities and follow up on them. Only use the TV or videos as a baby-sitter for short periods of time. Never allow televisions or computers in children's bedrooms. Know which TV programs, websites, and video games are child appropriate. Watch TV with children for at least one-half of their allotted time to see what they are watching, and set limits on both computers and televisions.

Monitor Music and Rap Music

Some types of music tend to glorify violence and hatred. It can instigate anger that if acted upon may turn to rage. These influences tend to make violence seem commonplace. Children may assume it's the way most people solve problems when they get older. While temper tantrums can be normal, rages are violent attacks and not something that will pass with age. Parents should instill morals and values, but sometimes they hesitate to do so because it takes too much time and effort, and they want their limited time together to be fun.
Some parents are intimidated by their child. Some parents don't believe in discipline. A parent may avoid discipline because as a child, they were harshly disciplined.
Anger and aggression are normal in adults as well as children. However, they can be dangerous if not controlled. Be aware that children who turn to violence show a common desire for defiance against authoritative figures and law enforcement, rough justice, social control, self help, materialism, social identity, power, and achieving and maintaining high social status.

Bullies

The definition of a "bully" is a child or groups of children who repeatedly hurt, frighten, or harass others. They are everywhere—at work, home, and school. Bullies may appear tough by showing no sympathy toward their intended targets. They also may carry a weapon or bring it to school. They often make fun of a child's academic status, race, gender, living conditions, or the family's financial situation.

They tease, name call, threaten, curse, or use abusive language, and insult others. Bullies often steal someone else's property and have a past history of disciplinary problems. They tend to be older than the victim, males, confident, and/or irrational. Often they come from homes that lack parental supervision, and possibly from an abusive home. They generally victimize only when adults are not around.

Bully Proof Children

Talk to your children about bullying. Explain that teasing others is wrong and not acceptable behavior. Ask how they would feel if someone teased them frequently. Demonstrate self-protection skills by staying alert, helping them to know where to go for help and how to walk with confidence. Teach your child ways to resolve arguments without violent words or actions.

Conclusion

Shreveport, like any other major city, is not exempt from crime. Crime has been around since the beginning of time and isn't going away anytime soon. With new technology, opportunities to educate ourselves about crime prevention and good sense, women have many tools at their disposal with which to stay alive and healthy. We eat food that is sugar-free and low in calories. We look for the best bargains, hunt for that appropriate mate, and do our best to raise obedient children. Why shouldn't we live to enjoy all the good things God has made available to us?

It has been said that a wise man learns from the mistakes of others while a fool learns from his own mistakes. Please learn from the women and girls of this book who died so brutally. They can't come back and tell us, "I shouldn't have gone down that dark street alone," or, "I could have dressed more appropriately in the first place." Every situation is different. There is no one magic maneuver that will save you. If you scream, the criminal could run away, or he could go ahead and kill or rape you. If you give in, he could let you go when he's through with you or he could kill you.

In the criminal world there are no absolutes. I've seen a person who was shot in the head live, and I've seen a person shot in the leg who died. The will to live is weaker in some people, and they convince themselves that they are going to die, especially if they see a lot of blood. A strong will to live does make a big difference in a person's chances for survival. People with a strong will to live perform incredible feats because they believe they have nothing to lose but their life!

If you have fallen down in hopelessness following a violent incident against you, no matter how low you are, you can get back up again. Try with all your power and might to overcome the situation. Romans 8:37 says, "Yet in all these things we are more than conquerors through Him who loved us." Think before getting into another bad situation. It's like spilled milk. There's nothing you can do to change the situation and undo what has been done. It's over. Try to accept it and go on.

Continue to appreciate the Azaleas and their vibrant colors along with the other beauties of the world, like your family. One day the memory of that tragic event will lessen and become bearable. The times of discouragement will become shorter. Your troubles and turmoil will make you less trusting, but that's good. Soon you won't think of the incident so often. If you let go a little each day, it will finally let you go.

Not Again!

Don't let yourself think that because it happened once you are free from tragedy or that the same thing can't happen to you again. That's what Alexis thought. She and her husband lost their oldest of two sons in an automobile accident. She could not quite get over it. Their son was a good Christian child, and they all went to church together as a family and did what was right.

The younger son needed his mother now more than ever because he'd lost his only brother, friend, and role model. Alexis wanted to grieve on her own and in her own time. She did not attend to the needs of the younger son, thinking he'd be fine. She just wanted him to leave her alone in her grief.

Within one year of the oldest son's death, the youngest and only remaining child was tragically killed.

I Can't See the Azaleas
True Crimes Against Women and Children

She was overwhelmed and distraught. Only then did she realize that losing her first son to tragedy did not exempt her from having it happen again.

Just because something like being raped or beaten has happened to you once does not mean that you're exempt from it happening again. Be careful, cautious, safe, and love yourself and your family.

Don't be fooled into thinking that pretty, young, old, rich, or ugly have an exemption from crime or bodily harm. You can become a target and a statistic and leave your family to deal with the traumatic aftermath of mourning your death.

Where there is little caution, there is much torment. Forethought means to be protected in advance. Study a matter carefully, decide what steps to take, and take them. Don't allow fear to keep you from adventure. However, make sure you are moving in the right direction for the right reason.

My friend and Bible study minister, Kathy, says, "As long as you're still breathing there is still a chance to be something you might have been." Kathy has taught me much in the last years, and it enables me to teach and help others. Because we have been given such an abundant benevolence—sheltered and fed with God's good care—we have learned to share our endowment with every person that we see.

We try to help those who need our support. We cannot see another's lack and not share. Whether it's our glowing fire, a loaf of bread, a sheltered roof over their head, we give so they too may be comforted. Wealth is not meant to be hoarded. It is meant to be shared with those in need. Perhaps through our giving, a family can be spared hardships and sometimes even brutality in the home. It may cause someone to become a trustworthy citizen in society instead of a menace to society. Instead of becoming a murderer or a rapist, perhaps someone will become a minister or a radiologist.

You don't have to go out and look for a suffering or a struggling family. If you aren't too busy looking down on them, you'll notice they've been placed in your path. I hope you will help and share with them the love and shelter that has been lavished upon you. As you count your blessings, remember to thank the Blesser.

As your cup runs over, acknowledge that God lent a hand in the filling, and then place the overrun in trust for the benefit of others. Show someone that their life can be as vibrant as an Azalea, and that they must simply possess the will to live and persevere through the struggle.

What is bitter to endure is sweet to conquer. The achievement is more pleasant because the struggle was so trying. When you have overcome a tribulation, praise God for those who have encouraged you. Recall those special individuals who offered a helping hand or an encouraging word when you really needed it. Thank God for them.

Keep in mind, thousands of people have lost their lives because they made that final mistake of being too careless. We should be grateful that we have life. Life is meant to be lovely, and we should avoid the dangers such as unforgiveness, hate, envy, vengeance, spite, pride, meddlesomeness, and selfishness that can mar our loveliness. They should be chased away with thoughtfulness, bigheartedness, kindness, love, forgiveness, tolerance, humility, and goodwill.

We are meant to be happy. Life has its problems. Don't add to them by making pathetic and inattentive choices.

Whether it's a physical, mental, or financial struggle, always do what's right. Uncontrollable circumstances can have a bearing on you, but the will to live and the wisdom to strive will carry you a long way.

I Can't See the Azaleas
True Crimes Against Women and Children

Live to see the beauty of the Azaleas, for that's what life is all about: God's Beauty.

photo by Roger Courtney

About the Author

Dianna Cook Thomas has been a police officer for more than 12 years. She was also a Police Jailer for one year. She received a B.A. degree in Health and Physical Education from Centenary College of Louisiana, a Methodist college, and a Master's degree in Industrial/Organizational Psychology from Louisiana Tech University in Ruston, Louisiana.

While on the police department, she advanced herself by becoming an FBI Instructor, a Physical Fitness Certified Instructor, a Domestic Violence Instructor, a Sexual Harassment Instructor, a Firearms Instructor, Armorer Certified, and Defensive Tactics Instructor.

Dianna has been honored for several community service awards, and has received numerous commendation letters from her supervisors for her commitment and dedication to serving the citizens of Shreveport, Louisiana.

Made in the USA
San Bernardino, CA
04 March 2019